THE 30-MINUTE GLUTEN-FREE COOKBOOK

THE 30-MINUTE GLUTEN-FREE COOKBOOK

100+ QUICK AND SIMPLE RECIPES FOR EVERY DAY

Jan Withington

Photography by Evi Abeler

ROCKRIDGE
PRESS

For general information on our other products and services or to obtain technical support, please contact our Customer Care Department within the United States at (866) 744-2665, or outside the United States at (510) 253-0500.

Rockridge Press publishes its books in a variety of electronic and print formats. Some content that appears in print may not be available in electronic books, and vice versa.

Interior and Cover Designer: John Clifford
Art Producer: Michael Hardgrove
Editor: Lauren Moore
Production Editor: Nora Milman

Cover: Skillet Veggie Lasagna , page 62

ISBN: Print 978-1-64611-825-0 | eBook 978-1-64611-826-7

RO

THIS BOOK IS DEDICATED
TO MY HUSBAND, BILL,
MY SONS, BRANDON AND JACOB,
MY EXTENDED FAMILY IN NEW YORK,
MY SISTER, JOVY,
AND MY IN-LAWS.

CONTENTS

INTRODUCTION viii

CHAPTER ONE: AN INTRODUCTION TO THE GLUTEN-FREE LIFE 1

CHAPTER TWO: BREAKFAST AND SMOOTHIES 11

CHAPTER THREE: SOUPS AND SALADS 23

CHAPTER FOUR: SNACKS AND SIDES 35

CHAPTER FIVE: VEGETARIAN AND VEGAN MAINS 53

CHAPTER SIX: SEAFOOD MAINS 71

CHAPTER SEVEN: POULTRY MAINS 83

CHAPTER EIGHT: MEAT MAINS 101

CHAPTER NINE: DESSERTS AND SWEET TREATS 119

CHAPTER TEN: SEASONINGS, SAUCES, AND STAPLES 131

SAMPLE MENUS 142

MEASUREMENT CONVERSIONS 145

RESOURCES 146

INDEX 147

INTRODUCTION

I grew up in the Philippines, where my family and I lived a modest life. My father was a police deputy in our town, but with five children attending school at the same time, we rarely bought expensive treats like pastries, cakes, breads, or other baked goods. We mainly ate rice, fish, and lots of fruits and vegetables. I was a healthy child, and I don't remember having digestive issues back then.

About 20 years ago, I moved to the United States and married my husband. Not long after, I started having gastrointestinal symptoms. I tried to ignore them most of the time, but they started to interfere with the things I wanted to do. My stomach issues were making me feel sick all the time, I didn't have a lot of energy, my sleep was very bad, and I started getting skin rashes and breakouts. I went to see a doctor, who referred me to an immunologist. I was given allergy skin tests, but I wasn't tested for gluten sensitivity. My doctor gave me allergy pills that I took on and off, but the pain in my stomach never went away.

After seeing multiple doctors and specialists who couldn't work out what was happening, I felt like a hypochondriac. But then, after watching TV shows about health issues, I heard about gluten and why some people cannot eat it. Researching gluten sensitivities and conditions like celiac, I learned about the symptoms, treatments, testing, and so on. Eventually I figured out I had mild celiac disease–like symptoms and made the connection to the food I was eating.

I tried to figure out which products might be loaded with gluten—sauces, condiments, baked goods, snacks, drinks, chocolates, and plenty of other foods. After deciding to avoid a lot of foods, I went back to my usual Filipino diet of mostly white rice, fish, chicken, and veggies. Within two weeks, my stomachache disappeared.

Once I began reading labels on products at the grocery store, I realized it's not always easy to figure out which products are gluten-free, so I decided to research gluten-free products on the internet. At that time, there weren't a lot of them on the market.

Cooking was a challenge for the first six months or so. Not only did I have to come up with a meal for myself, I had to come up with another for my husband and two boys. They didn't like gluten-free food, as it wasn't as tasty or flavorful as the regular American food they were used to. It was tiring and I was exhausted. Eventually, I decided to cook gluten-free meals that everybody could enjoy. I experimented in my kitchen, creating meals that were easy to make, but also gluten-free and delicious.

I decided to share what I learned—how to make tasty, gluten-free food that everyone could enjoy—on my blogs, TheGlutenFree.com and GlutenFreeByJan.com.

I understand how busy our lives can get. We don't always have a lot of time to spend in the kitchen preparing meals—and sometimes, we just don't want to! The good news is that gluten-free cooking doesn't need to be complicated.

This cookbook contains easy gluten-free recipes for busy people who are running around every day, with jobs, families, friends, and other responsibilities. It's full of simple, delicious, and healthy recipes that anybody can prepare in 30 minutes—and in some cases, even less.

I hope you'll find this book helpful, and that it makes your gluten-free life easier and happier.

CHAPTER ONE

AN INTRODUCTION TO THE GLUTEN-FREE LIFE

The challenges of following a restrictive diet can be overwhelming. I know—I've been there. When I was diagnosed with gluten sensitivity, I was devastated. At that time, gluten-sensitivity awareness was still pretty new and there weren't a lot of gluten-free food alternatives. I didn't really know what to eat or where to start. Now, there are more choices. The selection can be varied, and there are some fantastic gluten-free alternatives to gluten-filled foods. It's a lot easier now! The key is knowing what you're dealing with.

< Sheet-Pan Chicken Fajitas, page 91

WHAT IS GLUTEN, AND WHY CAN'T SOME PEOPLE EAT IT?

Gluten is a protein that exists in wheat, rye, spelt, and barley. It's found in ingredients for a wide range of commercially available foods. Flour alone is present in thousands of products because it gives products consistency and structure and assists in thickening foods like salad dressings, soups, and sauces.

People react differently to gluten. Some people have no trouble processing it, while others do. If people who don't know they are sensitive to gluten continue to consume it, it creates physiological reactions that result in inflammation. These symptoms may include fatigue, bloating, constipation, diarrhea, headaches, skin problems, depression, and joint pain.

There are many reasons why some people can't eat food that contains gluten, but some people choose to limit their gluten intake as a matter of personal preference. It's important to remember that all major diet changes should be made with the guidance of a qualified health care professional, who can ensure you're getting all the required nutrition that your body needs to function. It's also important to be careful that you don't deprive yourself of needed nourishment. For people who don't have a medical condition, eating a gluten-free diet isn't necessarily healthier than a diet containing gluten products.

Gluten Sensitivity and Celiac Disease

There are varying degrees of gluten sensitivity. One of the most serious is an autoimmune disease called celiac disease. In people with celiac disease, ingesting gluten leads to damage to their small intestines. Their immune systems attack the villi, which are small, fingerlike projections lining the small intestine that promote nutrient absorption. Damaged villi make it nearly impossible for the body to absorb nutrients, leading to malnourishment and other health issues.

The National Celiac Association estimates that 1 in 133 Americans—or about 1 percent of the population—has celiac disease. If you suspect that you or someone in your family has celiac disease, it's important to get tested by a medical professional. Celiac disease can develop at any age after people start eating foods or medicines that contain gluten.

If left undiagnosed or untreated, celiac disease can lead to serious health problems. The primary treatment of celiac disease is eliminating gluten in the diet.

Keep in mind that not everyone with a sensitivity to gluten also has celiac. Always remember that it's important to seek out a diagnosis from a medical professional if you suspect you may have celiac disease.

GUIDELINES FOR THE GLUTEN-FREE LIFE

Switching to a gluten-free diet can be challenging. It requires planning, carefully reading labels, and checking hidden sources of gluten. Here are some essential tips to follow when you are on a gluten-free diet.

Know the Basic Gluten-Free Grains and Alternatives

While all wheat-based foods (so long, pasta) and some grains are no-gos, there are a lot of naturally gluten-free grains you can enjoy.

- **Corn:** This staple food for many people around the world is great as a gluten-free substitute.
- **Millet:** Technically a seed, millet is popular in baking gluten-free bread.
- **Quinoa:** These gluten-free seeds are great for grain-based dishes.
- **Rice:** All types of rice, including wild rice, are fine to eat if you have a gluten sensitivity.
- **Sorghum:** This gluten-free cereal grain is a great substitute for wheat flour.
- **Teff:** An ancient grain about the size of a poppy seed, teff can be eaten whole or ground into a gluten-free flour alternative.

Check Your Labels

Reading the labels for food, drinks, and even toiletries is so important when you're living with a food allergy or intolerance. In addition to checking for obvious ingredients like wheat, barley, malt, and rye, look for certified gluten-free labels. The Food and Drug Administration only allows products with less than 20 parts per million (ppm) of gluten to be labeled as gluten-free.

Some products are naturally gluten-free but may be manufactured in a facility that processes wheat or other glutinous products. If the label says something like "manufactured in a facility with wheat" or "may contain wheat," it's best to steer clear.

Another important thing to be aware of is recalled products. Sometimes manufacturers make mistakes, especially if their facilities also manufacture products with gluten. The good news is that companies usually disclose if they have a recalled product, so keep up with news updates as much as possible.

Sneaky Sources of Gluten

It's essential to always check a product's labels and ingredients list—especially if you've been diagnosed with celiac disease. There are hidden sources that can be harder to recognize, especially because gluten is used for fillers and thickeners in many products. Check the following list for some of these products.

- **Canned soups:** Similar to condiments, thickening agents that contain gluten are sometimes used in canned soups—especially the creamy ones.
- **Chocolate:** Pure, unsweetened chocolate is naturally gluten-free, as is quality, commercially available chocolate made with simple ingredients like cocoa butter and sugar. But some brands contain additional ingredients like flavoring agents or emulsifiers that can contain gluten.
- **Condiments:** Salad dressings, marinades, gravies, and other sauces will sometimes use products containing gluten as a thickening agent.
- **Processed meats:** Even though the meat itself is, of course, gluten-free, processed meats like cold cuts, bacon, or sausage may contain flavorings or additives with gluten.
- **Spices and seasonings:** Most individual herbs and spices don't contain gluten, but some spice blends are combined with ingredients that contain gluten, such as wheat flour or starch.

Prevent Cross-Contamination

The first thing I did when I was diagnosed with a gluten sensitivity was clean my kitchen. I scrubbed all the appliances, cutting boards, pizza slicers, can openers, spatulas, strainers, and colanders. I separated plates, utensils, cups, and others for myself in one corner of my kitchen. If your entire family isn't going gluten-free, it's important to have designated gluten-free areas in your kitchen, and gluten-free kitchen supplies—especially if someone in the family has celiac disease. Cross-contamination is no joke.

Eventually, I decided to go completely gluten-free with my family and tried to come up with decent gluten-free food every day for everybody to enjoy.

Cross-contamination can happen when you're out and about, too. Going out to eat is a red flag for me. Even now, I still worry about getting sick when I'm at a restaurant. Fortunately, there are some good apps to help people with gluten sensitivity find safe places to eat. I recommend Find Me Gluten-Free, which lists gluten-free-friendly restaurants near a user's location. It also features customer reviews, which can help you decide what's best for you and your family.

Eat Naturally Gluten-Free Foods

While it's easy to slip into focusing on all the things you can't eat anymore when you're diagnosed with a gluten sensitivity, there are so many delicious things you can still enjoy. A gluten-free diet will be much healthier if you focus on whole foods that are naturally gluten-free, including fresh meats, fresh fish, gluten-free grains, fruits, vegetables, beans, and more.

If you love gardening like I do, it can be a good idea to grow your own herbs like rosemary, sage, parsley, thyme, basil, oregano, cilantro, and so many others. After the summer months, I dry the herbs and store them in nicely labeled containers. They're good for up to one year.

Simple Swaps

When you're living with a gluten sensitivity, you have to think outside the box when it comes to food. Here are some swaps you can make that can help you embrace the gluten-free lifestyle a little easier.

Arrowroot: This can be used as a thickener for sauces, as well as baking breads and desserts.

Cassava flour: This flour is different from tapioca flour. It's made from the whole roots, and simply peeled, dried, and ground. It's a good substitute for wheat flour in baking.

Coconut flour: Made from dried coconut meat, this is good for baking breads and desserts.

Corn tortillas: While flour tortillas are a no-go for people with gluten sensitivities, you can still enjoy tacos with all the fixings piled into a corn tortilla.

Nut flours: Almond flour and cashew nuts are good substitutes in gluten-free baking.

Potato starch: This can replace cornstarch in baking or be used as a thickener in soups, sauces, and stews.

Tapioca flour: A starch extracted from the cassava root, this is a good gluten-free, grain-free, and nut-free option as a thickener, and you can also use it for baking breads.

GLUTEN-FREE MADE EASY

Many people don't have the time or inclination to cook elaborate meals every day—or even once in a while. When you throw a food intolerance into the mix, cooking might start to feel like a dreaded chore.

That's where this book comes in handy. It's full of gluten-free recipes that can be prepared in 30 minutes or less and are simple to follow. I like simple and easy recipes—but, of course, they also have to be delicious. This collection of recipes is specifically tailored for hassle-free gluten-free cooking. I hope you use this book as your go-to source for wonderful gluten-free dishes any day of the week. Cooking gluten-free doesn't have to be a pain—you can prepare quick, delicious meals without stressing.

I have a variety of recipes in this book, from smoothies to salads, soups to sweets, and mouth-watering main dishes for everybody to enjoy. Gluten-free dishes don't need to be bland, boring, or difficult. They can be fun, tasty, and easy. I've also included descriptions indicating whether they are vegetarian or vegan, or if they're also safe for people suffering from other common allergies such as peanuts and tree nuts, dairy, and soy. This should help you decide which of these tasty dishes you'd like to make for yourself or your family.

Remember: You don't have to do it all. As you shop, be aware of the resources around you. Take advantage of precut or frozen fruits and veggies, which can save you precious prep time. And if you really want to save time cooking, you can double up on these recipes so that you have leftovers that can be reheated later.

With more than 100 step-by-step recipes, this book will give you plenty of inspiration in the kitchen. And you can easily make substitutions to turn the recipes into your new favorite meals.

Helpful Hacks

There are many tricks and techniques that can save you time in the kitchen. Take advantage of these clever kitchen gadgets you can use to save time prepping.

- **Food processor:** The metal blade chops and mixes, while attachment disks shred and grate. The more expensive the processor, the more sophisticated the jobs it will do. Some even come with a mini bowl for smaller quantities.
- **Handheld electric mixer:** Using one of these is much faster than whisking and mixing by hand.
- **Multifunctional vegetable chopper/slicer:** These are inexpensive gadgets that will help you when you are prepping, from slicing potatoes to chopping carrots and zucchini.
- **Pressure cooker:** This handy tool cuts short your cooking time by up to two-thirds. Be sure to check out my recipe for Pressure Cooker Beef Stew (page 112).

Equipment and Essentials

These are some kitchen essentials that make gluten-free cooking easier that I recommend keeping on hand:

- **Food processor:** Say goodbye to chopping, blending, dicing, and slicing by hand. Food processors are a great way to cut down on food prep, especially if you find yourself cutting up lots of vegetables.
- **Handheld electric mixer:** A hand mixer is helpful for cooking both savory and sweet dishes. The attachments are also super easy to clean.
- **Instant thermometers:** How do you know if your meat is done? Cutting into a pork chop or steak isn't ideal—and eyeballing it isn't always the safest bet. An instant thermometer is critical for food safety.
- **Mandoline:** When you're making a dish that requires a very thinly sliced ingredient, you'll want a mandoline. Be careful using this one, though—the blades are very sharp, and it's easy to cut your finger.
- **Sheet pans:** These are key for roasting vegetables, toasting nuts, or baking cookies. They come in a bunch of different sizes, so decide which one works best for your oven.
- **Vegetable peeler:** If you ever prep potatoes, carrots, cucumbers, zucchini, parsnips, or any other vegetable with a skin you'd rather not eat, a vegetable peeler is key.

Pantry Staples

It's well worth stocking up on products you know are certified gluten-free to help cut down on prep time. Here are some of the pantry items that I usually keep around for my own gluten-free cooking.

- Almond meal and flour
- Beans
- Broth—chicken, beef, and vegetable
- Flour blend, gluten-free
- Nuts and seeds
- Oats, gluten-free
- Olive oil, extra-virgin
- Pasta, gluten-free
- Polenta
- Quinoa
- Rice
- Rice noodles
- Spices
- Taco kits
- Tamari or gluten-free soy sauce
- Tomato sauce

Common Food Allergies and Substitutions

If gluten is your only food intolerance, congratulations! Unfortunately, it's common for people with food allergies to have more than one. Here are some of the most common food allergies as well as ideas for substitutions.

Eggs: You can experiment with alternatives and find what works best for you. I've found that applesauce, mashed banana, ground flax seeds or chia seeds, silken tofu, yogurt, buttermilk, and arrowroot powder are great options.

Fish and shellfish: If you are allergic to fish or shellfish, you can get your daily dose of protein from grass-fed meat, organic chicken, or black beans. To get the benefits from the nutrients found in fish, opt for leafy green vegetables or flaxseed oil.

Milk/dairy: People with a dairy allergy often have an adverse reaction to lactose, so try swapping out dairy products with lactose-free alternatives. Fortunately, there are a lot of dairy-free milks available these days, including coconut milk, soy milk, rice milk, almond milk, and oat milk.

Peanuts: If the only nut you're allergic to is peanuts, feel free to replace peanuts with almonds or cashews. The most common peanut butter alternative is almond butter, which contains healthy fats and proteins. You can also swap in seeds such as pumpkin and sunflower seeds. Sunflower seed butter is a good alternative for recipes that call for peanut butter.

Soy: When you have a soy allergy and a recipe calls for soy sauce or tamari, try coconut aminos.

Tree nuts: These include walnuts, cashews, Brazil nuts, hazelnuts, almonds, pistachios, and pecans. The best alternatives are sunflower seeds, pumpkin seeds, flaxseeds, and chia seeds.

CHAPTER TWO

BREAKFAST AND SMOOTHIES

Hawaiian Smoothie Bowl 12

Lean and Green Smoothie 13

Berry-Chia Yogurt Parfait 14

Baked Avocado Egg Boats 15

Egg Muffins 16

Vegetable Frittata 17

Bacon and Cheese Frittata 18

Belgian Waffles 19

Berry Crepes 20

Quick Sausage Cornmeal Pancakes 21

< Baked Avocado Egg Boats, page 15

HAWAIIAN SMOOTHIE BOWL

VEGETARIAN, SOY-FREE

Serves 4 :: Prep time: 10 minutes

Fruity and delicious, this smoothie bowl is full of summery tropical flavors that you can enjoy anytime. Top with your favorite fresh fruits and gluten-free granola, and you're all set.

2 ripe bananas

1½ cups frozen mango

1½ cups frozen pineapple

1 cup plain Greek yogurt

¼ cup almond milk (add as needed)

TOPPING OPTIONS

Fresh berries, toasted unsweetened coconut flakes, sliced kiwi, gluten-free granola

1. Combine the ingredients in a blender. Blend on high until smooth.
2. If the mixture is too thick, add a little bit of almond milk.
3. Pour into a serving bowl and top with your favorite fruits.

Per serving: Total calories: 161; Total fat: 2g; Carbohydrates: 31g; Fiber: 3g; Sugars: 22g; Protein: 7g

LEAN AND GREEN SMOOTHIE

VEGAN, DAIRY-FREE, NUT-FREE, SOY-FREE

Makes 4 cups :: Prep time: 10 minutes

The fastest way to up your intake of fruits and veggies is to blend them into a smoothie. This one is so crisp and delicious!

1 Granny Smith apple

2½ cups baby kale

1 cup pineapple chunks

1 cup apple juice, chilled

½ cup green grapes, frozen

1. Peel, core, and chop the apple.
2. Place all the ingredients in a blender.
3. Cover and blend until smooth.

Recipe tip: If you're not a fan of kale, baby spinach is a good substitute.

Per serving (1 cup): Total calories: 107; Total fat: 1g; Carbohydrates: 26g; Fiber: 4g; Sugars: 18g; Protein: 2g

BERRY-CHIA YOGURT PARFAIT

VEGETARIAN, SOY-FREE

Makes 6 cups :: Prep time: 10 minutes

This is a great breakfast that will keep you feeling full all morning. Chia seeds are a good source of omega-3 fatty acids and fiber, and they can help lower cholesterol.

2 cups mixed fresh berries, divided

1 tablespoon agave nectar, divided

3 cups plain yogurt

1 cup gluten-free granola

2 tablespoons chia seeds

1. In a large bowl, mix 1 cup of berries with ½ tablespoon of agave nectar and mash the berries to desired consistency. Add the remaining 1 cup of berries.
2. Combine the yogurt with the remaining ½ tablespoon of agave nectar in a medium bowl.
3. Spoon about 3 tablespoons of the yogurt mixture into six 8-ounce glasses. Top each glass with a few tablespoons of the berry mixture, and then sprinkle some of the granola and ½ teaspoon of chia seeds on top.
4. Repeat layers once.

Recipe tip: For an added protein boost, use Greek yogurt instead of plain.

Per serving (1 cup): Total calories: 191; Total fat: 6g; Carbohydrates: 26g; Fiber: 4g; Sugars: 17g; Protein: 9g

BAKED AVOCADO EGG BOATS

DAIRY-FREE, NUT-FREE, SOY-FREE

Serves 4 :: Prep time: 10 minutes :: Cook time: 12 to 15 minutes

Is there anything better than a perfectly ripe avocado? Maybe these egg-filled avocado boats. This filling, low-carb breakfast is loaded with healthy fats and protein. Feel free to top these with grated Cheddar cheese, diced scallions, or a dash of your favorite hot sauce.

4 slices bacon

2 ripe (semi-firm) avocados

4 large eggs

2 tablespoons finely chopped fresh chives

Salt

Freshly ground black pepper

1. Preheat the oven to 375°F.
2. Arrange the bacon strips on a paper towel–lined plate, and microwave until crispy, 3 to 5 minutes. Chop or crumble the bacon and set aside.
3. Slice the avocados in half and remove the pit. Scoop out about 2 tablespoons of avocado flesh to make the hole bigger to accommodate the egg. Place the avocados on an inverted muffin tin to keep them in place. Crack 1 egg into each avocado half and season with salt and pepper.
4. Bake for 12 to 15 minutes, or until eggs are set.
5. Garnish with the chives and crispy bacon.

Recipe tip: Make this vegetarian by omitting the bacon.

Per serving: Total calories: 260; Total fat: 21g; Carbohydrates: 8g; Fiber: 6g; Sugars: 1g; Protein: 12g

EGG MUFFINS

VEGETARIAN, NUT-FREE, SOY-FREE

Makes 12 muffins :: Prep time: 10 minutes :: Cook time: 20 minutes

These healthy egg muffins are so easy to prepare. Make them over the weekend—they'll be a great grab-and-go breakfast option for your family on weekday mornings when you've got to get to school or work.

- 1 tablespoon extra-virgin olive oil, plus more to grease the pan
- ½ cup finely chopped onion
- ¾ cup chopped cherry tomatoes
- 12 eggs
- 1 cup fresh baby spinach, roughly chopped
- ¼ cup milk
- Pinch salt
- Freshly ground black pepper
- 1 ripe but firm avocado, peeled, pitted, and diced (optional)
- Fresh salsa (optional)
- 3 to 4 tablespoons crumbled feta cheese (optional)

1. Preheat the oven to 350°F and grease a 12-muffin pan.
2. Heat the oil in a small pan over medium heat. Sauté the onions until soft and then add the tomatoes. Cook for a couple of minutes, or until the tomatoes start to soften. Remove the pan from the heat and let it cool slightly.
3. In a large bowl, whisk together the eggs, spinach, and milk. Stir in the onion-and-tomato mixture, and then season with salt and pepper.
4. Carefully fill the muffin pan, allowing about half an inch for the eggs to expand while cooking.
5. Bake for about 20 minutes, or until eggs are set. Remove from the oven and let the muffins cool for a few minutes. If desired, serve with avocado, salsa, and feta cheese.

Recipe tip: Feel free to get creative with the muffin veggie fillings. One option is to use chopped scallions, jalapeños, and cilantro instead of spinach and tomatoes.

Per serving (1 muffin): Total calories: 89; Total fat: 6g; Carbohydrates: 2g; Fiber: <1g; Sugars: 1g; Protein: 7g

VEGETABLE FRITTATA

VEGETARIAN, NUT-FREE, SOY-FREE

Serves 6 :: Prep time: 10 minutes :: Cook time: 20 minutes

This dish is great for feeding a crowd at brunch. It's super easy to make, and it's loaded with fresh, healthy vegetables. Be sure to serve this warm.

2 tablespoons butter

1 tablespoon extra-virgin olive oil

1 red bell pepper, thinly sliced

1 yellow bell pepper, thinly sliced

1 red onion, cut into thin wedges

1 small zucchini, cut lengthwise then cut diagonally

Salt

Freshly ground black pepper

2 garlic cloves, minced

3 or 4 scallions, chopped

12 large eggs

1 cup half and half

¼ cup shredded Parmesan cheese

1. Preheat the oven to 350°F.
2. On the stovetop, heat a large cast iron pan over medium-high heat. Heat the butter and oil, and then sauté the bell peppers, red onion, and zucchini. Season with salt and pepper. Add the garlic and scallions, and sauté for another minute. Set aside.
3. Whisk the eggs, half and half, and Parmesan, and season with salt and pepper.
4. Pour the egg mixture into the pan with the sautéed vegetables. Stir to mix, and then bake for about 20 minutes, or until the eggs are set. Serve warm.

Per serving: Total calories: 288; Total fat: 21g; Carbohydrates: 8g; Fiber: 2g; Sugars: 4g; Protein: 16g

BACON AND CHEESE FRITTATA

NUT-FREE, SOY-FREE

Serves 6 :: Prep time: 5 minutes :: Cook time: 25 minutes

When you're looking for something quick but satisfying, you can't go wrong with this simple frittata. It's perfect for brunch, too.

1 teaspoon extra-virgin olive oil

6 strips bacon

6 large eggs

1 cup whole milk

2 tablespoons butter

Salt

Freshly ground black pepper

¼ cup chopped scallions

1 cup shredded Cheddar cheese

1. Preheat the oven to 350°F.
2. Grease an 11-by-7-inch baking dish with the oil.
3. Cook the bacon halfway (you don't want to cook it all the way because you still need to bake it) in the microwave, for about 2 minutes, and then chop it into bits and set aside.
4. In a large bowl, whisk together the eggs, milk, and butter, and season with salt and pepper. Pour the mixture into the prepared baking dish. Sprinkle with the bacon, scallions, and cheese.
5. Bake for 25 minutes, or until the eggs are set.

Recipe tip: Turkey bacon is a good substitute for regular bacon if you don't eat pork.

Per serving: Total calories: 256; Total fat: 20g; Carbohydrates: 3g; Fiber: <1g; Sugars: 2g; Protein: 15g

BELGIAN WAFFLES

VEGETARIAN

Makes 5 waffles :: Prep time: 10 minutes :: Cook time: 20 minutes

I can't get enough of these waffles! They are my favorite breakfast on Sunday mornings. Keep in mind you'll need a waffle maker to make these—but, personally, I think it's worth the investment.

2¼ cups gluten-free baking flour

¼ cup granulated sugar

1½ teaspoons gluten-free baking powder

½ teaspoon baking soda

½ teaspoon salt

2 large eggs

1½ cups cold milk

3 tablespoons melted butter

1 teaspoon vanilla extract

Nonstick cooking spray

1. In a large bowl, combine the flour, sugar, baking powder, baking soda, and salt.
2. In a separate bowl, whisk the eggs, milk, butter, and vanilla. Pour the wet ingredients into the dry ingredients and stir to incorporate. If the batter seems too thick, add a little more milk.
3. Preheat the waffle maker and spray with the nonstick cooking spray. Pour about ½ cup of batter in the center of the waffle maker and use a spatula to spread it out and fill the grooves. Do not overfill—keep in mind that the waffle will expand as it cooks. Close and cook according to waffle maker's directions—usually between 3 to 5 minutes.
4. Serve with your favorite fruit, maple syrup, or butter.

Per serving (1 waffle): Total calories: 341; Total fat: 11g; Carbohydrates: 54g; Fiber: 5g; Sugars: 15g; Protein: 10g

BERRY CREPES

VEGETARIAN

Serves 4 :: Prep time: 10 minutes :: Cook time: 20 minutes

My younger son loves these crepes so much, especially with fresh blueberries, blackberries, and raspberries.

FOR THE CREPES

2 large eggs

¾ cup milk

½ cup water

1 cup gluten-free all-purpose flour

¼ teaspoon xanthan gum (leave out if your flour mix already has it)

3 tablespoons butter, melted

2 tablespoons granulated sugar

1 teaspoon pure vanilla extract

FOR THE BERRY FILLING

2 cups mixed berries

½ cup sugar

1 tablespoon cornstarch

FOR THE CREAM FILLING

1 cup heavy whipping cream

1 cup sugar

8 ounces cream cheese

1 teaspoon vanilla extract

TOPPING OPTIONS

Mixed fresh berries, powdered sugar

TO MAKE THE CREPES

1. Whisk the eggs in a large bowl, and then add the rest of the crepe ingredients and mix until smooth.
2. Heat a nonstick pan over medium-low heat. Pour ¼ cup of batter into the center of the pan. Pick up the pan and swirl it to spread the batter evenly, making a circle.
3. Cook over medium to medium-low heat for about 2 minutes, or until browned on the bottom.
4. Carefully flip the crepe over and cook the other side until golden brown. Repeat with the remaining batter. Stack the crepes on a plate and loosely cover with foil to keep them warm.

TO MAKE THE BERRY FILLING

Once the crepes are done, mix the ingredients for the berry filling in a small saucepan and heat on medium-low until bubbly, about 10 minutes. Remove from heat and set aside.

TO MAKE THE CREAM FILLING

Using a blender, whip the ingredients for the cream filling until thick and smooth, about 2 minutes.

TO ASSEMBLE THE CREPES

Place a crepe on a plate. Top with berry and cream fillings. Roll the crepe up and top with more berry filling and fresh fruit.

Recipe tip: Cut down on prep time by mixing the crepe ingredients with a handheld mixer.

Per serving: Total calories: 989; Total fat: 54g; Carbohydrates: 120g; Fiber: 6g; Sugars: 93g; Protein: 14g

QUICK SAUSAGE CORNMEAL PANCAKES

Serves 5 :: Prep time: 10 minutes :: Cook time: 20 minutes

These are a little bit denser than a regular pancake but just as delicious—believe me. The toasted pecans are loaded with healthy fats and protein to get your morning started.

- 1 package gluten-free breakfast sausages
- 1 cup cornmeal
- 1 cup gluten-free all-purpose flour
- 3 teaspoons gluten-free baking powder
- ½ teaspoon baking soda
- 1 teaspoon cinnamon
- ¼ teaspoon nutmeg
- ¼ teaspoon salt
- 1 cup apple cider
- ½ cup nonfat plain yogurt
- 1 egg
- 2 tablespoons maple syrup
- 1 teaspoon vanilla
- Butter, for greasing
- ½ cup toasted pecans
- Syrup, for serving

1. Cook the sausages according to the package directions and then chop into small pieces. Set aside.
2. In a large bowl, combine the cornmeal, flour, baking powder, baking soda, cinnamon, nutmeg and salt.
3. In another bowl, whisk together the apple cider, yogurt, egg, maple syrup, and vanilla.
4. Combine the wet and dry ingredients, including the sausages.
5. Heat a griddle or nonstick pan over medium heat. Coat the pan with butter and scoop about ⅓ cup of batter into the pan. Cook each pancake for about 3 minutes, until the bottom is lightly browned, then flip to cook the other side for another 3 minutes.
6. Top with the toasted pecans and serve with syrup.

Per serving: Total calories: 482; Total fat: 24g; Carbohydrates: 55g; Fiber: 6g; Sugars: 14g; Protein: 17g

CHAPTER THREE

SOUPS AND SALADS

Watermelon-Tomato Salad 24

Heirloom Tomato and Cucumber Salad with Peach Dressing 25

Chicken and Mango Salad in Lettuce Bowls 26

Quinoa Salad with Mango and Avocado 27

Minestrone Pasta Salad 28

Garden Gazpacho Soup 29

Old-Fashioned Potato Soup 30

Ham and Cheese Soup 31

Easy Taco Soup 32

Chicken and Wild Rice Soup 33

< Watermelon-Tomato Salad, page 24

WATERMELON-TOMATO SALAD

VEGETARIAN, NUT-FREE, SOY-FREE

Serves 4 :: Prep time: 10 minutes

I don't know about you, but I just can't get enough watermelon. When it is in season, I highly recommend trying this refreshing salad.

2 tablespoons extra-virgin olive oil

1½ tablespoons sherry vinegar

Pinch salt

Pinch freshly ground black pepper

3 cups heirloom tomato wedges (about 1½ pounds)

3 cups seedless watermelon, cut into 1-inch cubes

3 cups trimmed watercress

2 tablespoons chopped fresh basil

6 tablespoons feta cheese crumbles

1. In a small bowl, whisk together the oil, vinegar, salt, and pepper.
2. In a large bowl, combine the tomatoes, watermelon, watercress, and basil. Pour the dressing over the salad and gently toss to coat. Top with the feta cheese and serve.

Recipe tip: To make this vegan friendly, omit the feta cheese or swap in a vegan cheese alternative.

Per serving: Total calories: 165; Total fat: 11g; Carbohydrates: 17g; Fiber: 2g; Sugars: 11g; Protein: 5g

HEIRLOOM TOMATO AND CUCUMBER SALAD WITH PEACH DRESSING

VEGAN, DAIRY-FREE, NUT-FREE, SOY-FREE

Serves 4 :: Prep time: 15 minutes

Tomatoes and peaches are at their best during the summertime, making this, in my opinion, the ultimate summer salad.

FOR THE DRESSING

1 very ripe peach

3 tablespoons gluten-free red wine vinegar

1 tablespoon fresh thyme leaves, minced

1 teaspoon granulated sugar

5 to 6 tablespoons extra-virgin olive oil

FOR THE SALAD

2 pounds multicolored heirloom tomatoes, cut into ⅓-inch-thick slices

2 medium cucumbers, peeled, seeded, and cut diagonally

½ cup red onion, thinly sliced

Handful fresh basil leaves

Pinch kosher salt

Freshly ground black pepper

TO MAKE THE DRESSING

1. Peel and finely chop the peach. Discard the pit.
2. Whisk together the peach with the rest of the dressing ingredients in a bowl.

TO ASSEMBLE THE SALAD

3. Arrange the tomatoes on a platter and top with the cucumbers, red onions, and basil. Sprinkle with salt and pepper.
4. Pour the dressing over the vegetables and enjoy.

Per serving: Total calories: 231; Total fat: 18g; Carbohydrates: 18g; Fiber: 4g; Sugars: 11g; Protein: 3g

CHICKEN AND MANGO SALAD IN LETTUCE BOWLS

NUT-FREE

Serves 6 :: Prep time: 15 minutes :: Cook time: 5 minutes

If you have leftover chicken, this is an excellent way to use it. The sweet and savory flavors pair so well together in this low-carb salad.

1 cup frozen corn kernels

2 large heads Boston or Bibb lettuce

1 (15-ounce) can black beans, drained and rinsed

1½ cups skinless cooked chicken

1½ cups ripe mangos (about 2), peeled, pitted, and chopped

1 small cucumber, cut lengthwise and cut into ¼-inch pieces

¾ cup shredded Colby Jack cheese blend

½ cup red bell pepper, chopped

½ cup ranch dressing

1. Cook corn according to the package directions. Rinse in cold water and drain.
2. Cut the lettuce leaves at the base and pick the nice ones. Gently wash and pat them dry with paper towels.
3. Arrange the lettuce on a serving platter.
4. In a large bowl, combine all the ingredients except the lettuce. Toss gently to mix.
5. Spoon chicken mixture over the lettuce and serve.

Recipe tip: Buy presliced mangos from the grocery store to cut down on prep time.

Per serving: Total calories: 334; Total fat: 16g; Carbohydrates: 30g; Fiber: 6g; Sugars: 9g; Protein: 19g

QUINOA SALAD WITH MANGO AND AVOCADO

NUT-FREE, SOY-FREE

Serves 6 :: Prep time: 10 minutes :: Cook time: 20 minutes

Quinoa has gained popularity with nutritionists around the world. It is very versatile and packed with fiber and protein. This salad can be prepared ahead of time and kept in the refrigerator until you are ready to serve it.

FOR THE SALAD

1 cup dry quinoa

1 (14.5-ounce) can low-sodium chicken broth

¼ cup water

Pinch salt

1 (15-ounce) can black beans, drained and rinsed

1 ripe mango, peeled, pitted, and chopped

1 ripe but firm avocado, peeled, pitted, and chopped

1 red bell pepper, chopped

½ cup diced scallion

⅓ cup fresh cilantro, chopped

FOR THE DRESSING

3 tablespoons extra-virgin olive oil

3 tablespoons lime juice

2 teaspoons raw honey

½ teaspoon ground cumin

¼ teaspoon ground ginger

¼ teaspoon cayenne pepper

1. Rinse the quinoa several times. Transfer it to a medium pot with the broth and water, and then season it with the salt. Bring to a boil, and then reduce the heat to low and simmer for about 20 minutes. Let the quinoa cool.
2. While the quinoa is cooking, whisk the oil, lime juice, honey, cumin, ginger, and cayenne pepper in a small bowl.
3. In a large bowl, combine the cooked quinoa, black beans, mango, avocado, bell pepper, scallion, and cilantro. Pour in the dressing and gently toss to combine.

Recipe tip: Make this vegetarian by cooking the quinoa in vegetable broth instead of chicken broth.

Per serving: Total calories: 333; Total fat: 14g; Carbohydrates: 45g; Fiber: 8g; Sugars: 10g; Protein: 10g

MINESTRONE PASTA SALAD

VEGETARIAN, NUT-FREE

Serves 8 :: Prep time: 15 minutes :: Cook time: 10 minutes

If you love minestrone soup, then you will definitely love this salad version. It's really great as a side dish with steak or chicken.

- 1 (15-ounce) can kidney beans, rinsed and drained
- 1 (14.5-ounce) can chickpeas, rinsed and drained
- 1 (14.5-ounce) can diced tomatoes, drained
- 8 ounces gluten-free pasta
- 1 green bell pepper, chopped
- ⅔ cup Italian salad dressing
- ½ cup shredded Parmesan cheese
- 1 (2-ounce) can sliced black olives, drained
- 3 scallions, chopped
- Pinch salt
- Freshly ground black pepper

1. Cook pasta according to the package directions. Rinse with cold water, drain, and transfer to a large bowl.
2. Add all the other ingredients and toss to coat. Season with salt and pepper. Refrigerate until ready to serve.

Recipe tip: You can cut down on prep time by buying pre-chopped vegetables at the grocery store. You can find chopped onions, peppers, and more in the produce aisle.

Per serving: Total calories: 353; Total fat: 13g; Carbohydrates: 49g; Fiber: 8g; Sugars: 5g; Protein: 10g

GARDEN GAZPACHO SOUP

DAIRY-FREE

Serves 8 :: Prep time: 25 minutes

This is one of my favorite soups. It keeps well in the refrigerator for 3 days, so you can also make it ahead of time.

4 cups tomato juice

2 cups tomatoes, peeled, seeded, and chopped

1 cup chopped celery

1 cup seeded and chopped cucumber

1 cup chopped green bell pepper

½ cup chopped onion

2 tablespoons minced fresh parsley

2 garlic cloves, minced

1 tablespoon minced fresh chives

1 teaspoon gluten-free Worcestershire sauce

2 tablespoons vegetable oil

Pinch salt

Freshly ground black pepper

1. In a large bowl, combine all ingredients except the oil. Season with salt and pepper.
2. Refrigerate until ready to serve.
3. Stir in the oil just before serving.

Recipe tip: The easiest way to peel tomatoes is by boiling them. First, slice a shallow "X" at the bottom of the tomatoes. Boil them for 25 seconds and then put them in ice water. The skin should come right off.

Per serving: Total calories: 80; Total fat: 4g; Carbohydrates: 11g; Fiber: 2g; Sugars: 6g; Protein: 2g

OLD-FASHIONED POTATO SOUP

VEGETARIAN, NUT-FREE, SOY-FREE

Serves 4 :: Prep time: 5 minutes :: Cook time: 20 minutes

Say goodbye to canned soup! This hearty potato soup made from scratch is much healthier—and so tasty. It's good as a starter or a side dish, too.

4 medium baking potatoes (about 2 pounds), peeled and cut into ½-inch pieces

2 tablespoons butter

1 small yellow onion, diced

3 cups milk

Pinch celery salt

Pinch cayenne pepper

Pinch salt

2 tablespoons minced fresh parsley

1. Place the potatoes in a pot with enough water to cover them. Boil for about 10 minutes, or until tender.
2. In a skillet, melt the butter over medium heat. Add the onion and cook for about 5 minutes, or until soft. Set aside.
3. Drain the potatoes, return them to the pot, and mash them with a potato masher while they are still warm.
4. Add the onion and scrape the remaining bits into the pot. Stir in the milk, celery salt, cayenne pepper, and salt.
5. Cook over medium heat, stirring frequently, for about 5 minutes. Make sure not to let the milk boil.
6. Ladle the soup into bowls and serve garnished with the parsley.

Recipe tip: Sometimes I top this soup with chopped crispy bacon because I can just never get enough bacon. You can also top this with shredded cheese, chives, scallions, or a dollop of sour cream.

Per serving: Total calories: 290; Total fat: 8g; Carbohydrates: 46g; Fiber: 6g; Sugars: 11g; Protein: 10g

HAM AND CHEESE SOUP

Serves 6 :: Prep time: 10 minutes :: Cook time: 20 minutes

Your favorite sandwich is now a soup. Easy and quick to make, this one is a real crowd-pleaser.

- 1 large russet potato, peeled and cubed
- 4 tablespoons unsalted butter, divided
- 8 ounces cooked ham, chopped
- 3 garlic cloves, minced
- 1 sweet onion, chopped
- ¼ cup all-purpose gluten-free flour
- 1 teaspoon dried thyme
- 4 cups low-sodium chicken broth
- 16 ounces finely chopped broccoli florets
- ¾ cup heavy cream
- 1½ cups shredded mild Cheddar cheese
- Pinch kosher salt
- Freshly ground black pepper

1. Put the potato cubes in a large, microwave-safe bowl. Fill with enough water to cover the potatoes and microwave until tender, about 6 minutes. Drain and set aside.
2. In a Dutch oven over medium heat, melt 1 tablespoon of butter. Add ham and cook for 3 to 4 minutes, stirring occasionally, until lightly browned. Transfer to a plate.
3. Melt the remaining 3 tablespoons of butter. Add the garlic and onion and cook for about 4 minutes, stirring occasionally, until translucent.
4. Whisk in the flour and thyme until lightly browned, about 1 minute. Stir in the broth, scraping any browned bits from the bottom of the Dutch oven. Bring to a slow boil, and then reduce the heat to simmer.
5. Stir in the potatoes. Using a potato masher, mash until the desired consistency is reached. Stir in the ham, broccoli, and heavy cream. Cover and simmer until the broccoli is tender, about 5 minutes.
6. Remove from heat. Gradually stir in the cheese until the soup is smooth, then season with salt and pepper.

Recipe tip: Sometimes thickening agents that contain gluten are added to store-bought stocks and broths. Always check your label to make sure the broth you're buying is certified gluten-free.

Per serving: Total calories: 422; Total fat: 29g; Carbohydrates: 22g; Fiber: 3g; Sugars: 4g; Protein: 17g

EASY TACO SOUP

NUT-FREE

Serves 6 :: Prep time: 10 minutes :: Cook time: 20 minutes

This easy-to-make soup is a taco in a bowl. Filled with ground beef, veggies, and taco seasoning, it's perfectly healthy and filling.

1 pound lean ground beef

2 tablespoons extra-virgin olive oil

1 small onion, finely chopped

2 garlic cloves, minced

1 (16-ounce) can kidney beans, drained and rinsed

2 cups beef broth

1½ cups chopped tomatoes

1 cup corn

1 red bell pepper, chopped

1 package (1-ounce) store-bought taco seasoning

TOPPING OPTIONS

Shredded cheese, sour cream, chopped onion, chopped jalapeño, cilantro, corn chips, lime wedges

1. In a medium pan, brown the meat and drain. Set aside.
2. Heat the oil in a Dutch oven over medium heat, then add the the onions and garlic and sauté for a few minutes. Add the beef, beans, broth, tomatoes, corn, bell pepper, and taco seasoning. Stir and simmer for about 15 minutes.
3. Serve with your favorite toppings.

Recipe tip: You can swap out the ground beef and use ground turkey instead if you're trying to limit your red meat intake.

Per serving: Total calories: 295; Total fat: 12g; Carbohydrates: 25g; Fiber: 5g; Sugars: 4g; Protein: 22g

CHICKEN AND WILD RICE SOUP

DAIRY-FREE, NUT-FREE

Serves 4 :: Prep time: 10 minutes :: Cook time: 20 minutes

Here's my spin on a traditional chicken and rice soup. Wild rice has more fiber and nutrients than white rice, and it's also delicious. This hearty soup makes a nutritious addition to any diet.

4 boneless, skinless chicken thighs

Pinch salt

Freshly ground black pepper

2 tablespoons extra-virgin olive oil

1 medium onion, chopped

4 celery stalks, chopped

4 medium carrots, chopped

2 (14.5-ounce) cans low-sodium chicken broth

1½ cups water

⅔ cup wild rice blend

1. Season the chicken with salt and pepper.
2. In a large pot or Dutch oven, heat the oil over medium-high heat. Lightly brown the chicken on both sides and transfer to a cutting board. Chop or shred the chicken into small pieces.
3. In the same Dutch oven, sauté the onions for 3 minutes, and then add the celery and carrots. Season with salt and pepper and cook for another 3 to 5 minutes.
4. Add the broth, water, rice, and chicken. Bring to a boil, then reduce to a simmer and cover.
5. Continue cooking the soup covered until the rice is tender, about 15 minutes.
6. Adjust the seasoning if needed and serve.

Recipe tip: To cut down on prep time, you can buy pre-chopped vegetables.

Per serving: Total calories: 311; Total fat: 15g; Carbohydrates: 26g; Fiber: 3g; Sugars: 5g; Protein: 20g

CHAPTER FOUR

SNACKS AND SIDES

Bacon-Wrapped Asparagus, Sweet Peppers, and Green Beans 36

Creamy Potato Salad 37

Bean Dip 38

Cucumber Cups with Sun-Dried Tomato and Cream Cheese 39

Confetti Tuna in Celery Sticks 40

Vegetable Dip 41

Baked Sweet Potato Wedges with Garlic Aioli 42

Vegetable Fritters 43

Pistachio Cranberry Energy Bites 44

Spicy Avocado Dip 45

Sweet-and-Sour Zucchini 46

No-Bake Protein Energy Balls 47

Apple Sandwiches with Almond Butter, Chocolate Chips, and Granola 48

Zucchini Pizza Bites 49

Roasted Corn on the Cob with Parmesan Cheese 50

< Bacon-Wrapped Asparagus, Sweet Peppers, and Green Beans, page 36

BACON-WRAPPED ASPARAGUS, SWEET PEPPERS, AND GREEN BEANS

DAIRY-FREE, NUT-FREE

Serves 6 :: Prep time: 5 minutes :: Cook time: 25 minutes

These bacon-wrapped veggies are a great snack or an hors d'oeuvre if you're hosting a dinner party.

3 tablespoons extra-virgin olive oil

1 tablespoon yellow mustard

1 pound asparagus, woody ends removed

¾ pound green beans, ends trimmed

2 bell peppers, cut into thin strips

1 pound bacon

Kosher salt

Freshly ground black pepper

1. Preheat the oven to 425°F.
2. In a small bowl, whisk the mustard and oil. Set aside.
3. Bring a pot of water to a boil. Add the asparagus and green beans and cook for 2 to 3 minutes, or until bright green and just tender. Drain and pat dry.
4. Make small bundles of the vegetables together. Wrap bacon around the middle of each bundle and place the ends of the bacon down on a baking pan.
5. Drizzle the mustard mixture over the vegetable bundles and season with salt and pepper.
6. Bake 20 to 25 minutes, broiling for the last 1 to 2 minutes to make the bacon crispy.

Recipe tip: To remove the woody ends of asparagus, simply hold the asparagus firmly on both ends and bend it up away from you until the asparagus snaps.

Per serving: Total calories: 237; Total fat: 17g; Carbohydrates: 10g; Fiber: 4g; Sugars: 4g; Protein: 14g

CREAMY POTATO SALAD

VEGETARIAN, NUT-FREE

Serves 12 :: Prep time: 5 minutes :: Cook time: 20 minutes

I consider this a comfort food. Creamy, nutritious, and satisfying, this potato salad would be welcome at any picnic, potluck, or backyard barbecue.

FOR THE POTATO SALAD

4 eggs

1⅓ pounds small red potatoes, cut into 1-inch cubes

3 tablespoons apple cider vinegar

½ teaspoon salt

1 celery stalk, chopped

1 medium zucchini, chopped

8 scallions, chopped

FOR THE DRESSING

1 cup mayonnaise

¼ cup sour cream

2 teaspoons prepared horseradish

2 teaspoons yellow mustard

1 teaspoon sugar

¼ teaspoon freshly ground black pepper

1. Hard-boil the eggs for about 15 minutes, and then peel, chop, and set aside.
2. Place the potato cubes in a microwave-safe bowl and cover with water. Microwave until fork-tender, about 6 minutes. Drain and let them cool slightly, then sprinkle with the vinegar and salt, and toss to coat.
3. Add the eggs and the remaining salad ingredients and mix gently.
4. Mix the dressing ingredients in a bowl. Pour over the salad and gently toss to coat.

Recipe tip: Here's what I've found to be the easiest way to peel hardboiled eggs: Right after draining them from boiling, immediately shock them with cold water and gently shake them in the pot to crack the shells. Then simply peel off the shells.

Per serving: Total calories: 199; Total fat: 16g; Carbohydrates: 10g; Fiber: 2g; Sugars: 4g; Protein: 4g

BEAN DIP

VEGETARIAN, NUT-FREE, SOY-FREE

Serves 6 :: Prep time: 5 minutes :: Cook time: 20 minutes

Beans are hard to beat when it comes to protein and fiber. Serve this dip with gluten-free chips or fresh veggies.

- 1 (16-ounce) can gluten-free refried beans
- 1 (8-ounce) package cream cheese, softened
- ½ cup sour cream
- 3 scallions, thinly sliced, divided
- 2 tablespoons taco seasoning
- 1 cup shredded Cheddar cheese, divided
- 1 cup shredded pepper jack cheese, divided
- 2 jalapeños, finely chopped, divided
- Kosher salt
- Freshly ground black pepper
- ½ cup cherry tomatoes, quartered
- ¼ cup queso fresco, crumbled
- ¼ cup red onion, chopped

1. Preheat the oven to 350°F.
2. In a large bowl, combine the beans, cream cheese, sour cream, taco seasoning, ½ cup each of Cheddar and pepper jack cheese, and half of the scallions and jalapeño. Season with salt and pepper.
3. Transfer to an oven-safe dish and top with the remaining ½ cup of Cheddar and pepper jack cheese. Bake for about 20 minutes, or until the cheese has melted.
4. Garnish with the tomatoes, queso fresco, red onion, and the remaining scallions, and jalapeño.

Recipe tip: You can find queso fresco in the dairy aisle at most grocery stores. If your store doesn't have it, use crumbled cotija or feta cheese instead.

Per serving: Total calories: 424; Total fat: 31g; Carbohydrates: 19g; Fiber: 5g; Sugars: 4g; Protein: 17g

CUCUMBER CUPS WITH SUN-DRIED TOMATO AND CREAM CHEESE

VEGETARIAN, NUT-FREE, SOY-FREE

Serves 8 :: Prep time: 20 minutes

These cute cucumber cups are a healthy, satisfying snack. I love how the saltiness of the olives and richness of the sun-dried tomatoes pair with the freshness of the basil and cucumbers.

- 6 medium cucumbers
- 2 (8-ounce) packages cream cheese
- ½ cup oil-packed sun-dried tomatoes, coarsely chopped
- ¼ cup fresh basil, coarsely chopped
- ¼ cup kalamata olives, pitted and coarsely chopped
- 1 to 3 tablespoons chopped fresh chives, for garnish

1. Peel strips of skin from the cucumbers, leaving alternating strips of skin.
2. Cut the cucumbers into 1½-inch-thick rounds. Using a teaspoon, scoop out the seeds, forming a well in the middle of each round.
3. Combine the cream cheese, sun-dried tomatoes, basil, and olives. Process in a food processor until well blended.
4. Spoon the cream cheese filling into a pastry bag with a large tip. Pipe the filling into the cucumbers. Garnish with the chives.

Recipe tip: If you don't have a pastry bag, you can make something similar. Cut one of the corners of a sandwich bag, fill the bag with the cream cheese filling, and pipe it into the cucumber cups.

Per serving: Total calories: 126; Total fat: 8g; Carbohydrates: 12g; Fiber: 3g; Sugars: 8g; Protein: 3g

CONFETTI TUNA IN CELERY STICKS

NUT-FREE, SOY-FREE

Serves 10 :: Prep time: 20 minutes

Celery is rich in vitamins A, C, and K, folate, potassium, and fiber. Aside from being super healthy, it makes a great crunchy vessel for this tuna salad.

- 1 (3-ounce) can chunk light tuna
- ½ cup shredded carrots
- ½ cup shredded red cabbage
- ¼ cup shredded zucchini
- 3 tablespoons cream cheese, softened
- 1 tablespoon plain yogurt
- ½ teaspoon dried basil, crushed
- Kosher salt
- Freshly ground black pepper
- 1 bunch celery, cut into 4-inch sticks

1. In a medium bowl, combine the tuna, carrots, cabbage, and zucchini.
2. Stir in the cream cheese, yogurt, and basil, and season with salt and pepper.
3. Spread the mixture into the celery sticks and serve.

Per serving: Total calories: 38; Total fat: 2g; Carbohydrates: 4g; Fiber: 2g; Sugars: 2g; Protein: 3g

VEGETABLE DIP

VEGETARIAN, NUT-FREE

Makes 2 cups :: Prep time: 10 minutes

This dip gets a nice kick from the salsa. It's a great snack to serve at parties or for kids to munch on after school while they do their homework.

- 1 cup sour cream
- ⅔ cup salsa
- ⅓ cup mayonnaise
- 2 tablespoons finely chopped scallions
- ¼ cup red bell pepper, finely chopped
- 1 teaspoon garlic salt
- Mixed vegetable dippers (about 4 to 5 cups): bell peppers, baby carrots, broccoli, cauliflower, grape tomatoes

1. In a medium bowl, combine sour cream, salsa, mayonnaise, scallions, bell pepper, and garlic salt.
2. Refrigerate until ready to serve.

Recipe tip: You could also serve this with gluten-free crackers or pita wedges or spread it on a sandwich in place of mayo.

Per serving (½ cup): Total calories: 278; Total fat: 25g; Carbohydrates: 8g; Fiber: 1g; Sugars: 9g; Protein: 3g

BAKED SWEET POTATO WEDGES WITH GARLIC AIOLI

VEGAN, DAIRY-FREE, SOY-FREE

Serves 4 :: Prep time: 10 minutes :: Cook time: 20 minutes

This is a quick, easy, foolproof way to bake sweet potatoes, and the dipping sauce is delicious. Cashews pair well with roasted vegetables—they blend up super creamy and oil-free—making this a great dip for vegans and omnivores alike.

FOR THE POTATO WEDGES

1 teaspoon extra-virgin olive oil, plus 2 tablespoons

3 large sweet potatoes

½ teaspoon Himalayan salt

1 teaspoon chipotle powder

FOR THE AIOLI

1 cup raw cashews

¾ cup water

3 or 4 garlic cloves

2 teaspoons Dijon mustard

Juice of ½ lemon

Pinch salt

TO MAKE THE POTATO WEDGES

1. Preheat the oven to 425°F.
2. Grease a baking pan with 1 teaspoon of oil.
3. Wash, peel, and pat dry the sweet potatoes. Remove the bad spots, and then cut the potatoes into long wedges no thicker than 1 inch. Drizzle with the remaining 2 tablespoons of oil and arrange them on the pan. Season with salt and lightly dust with the chipotle powder.
4. Bake for 20 minutes, turning a few times to cook evenly.

TO MAKE THE AIOLI

5. Place the ingredients in a blender or food processor and blend until creamy.
6. Adjust salt according to taste.

Recipe tip: If you don't have Himalayan salt, regular salt will work, too.

Per serving: Total calories: 378; Total fat: 22g; Carbohydrates: 37g; Fiber: 7g; Sugars: 13g; Protein: 8g

VEGETABLE FRITTERS

VEGETARIAN, DAIRY-FREE, NUT-FREE, SOY-FREE

Yield: 10 fritters :: Prep time: 15 minutes :: Cook time: 15 minutes

Fritters are an extremely popular roadside snack in South Asia. Here, we're using carrots, potatoes, and zucchini, but the veggie combo possibilities are endless. These would go great with Vegetable Dip (page 41) or simply dunked in ketchup.

- 1 large carrot, peeled
- 1 zucchini, peeled
- 1 russet potato, peeled
- 1 medium onion, halved and thinly sliced
- 2 teaspoons sea salt
- 2 large eggs
- Freshly ground black pepper
- ½ cup extra-virgin olive oil

1. Using a spiralizer, cut the carrot and zucchini.
2. Use a mandoline to slice the potato into thin strips.
3. In a colander, mix the carrot, zucchini, potato, and onion, and sprinkle with the salt. Let the vegetables stand for about 15 minutes. Pat dry with a paper towel.
4. In a separate bowl, whisk the eggs and season with pepper. Mix in the vegetables and stir to coat.
5. Heat a large sauté pan over medium-high heat. Add a splash of oil to the pan.
6. Scoop about ¼ cup of the vegetable mixture at a time and form thin patties that are about 3 inches in diameter. Drop the patties into the hot pan and fry for 2 to 3 minutes, until the fritters are golden brown and crisp. Flip and repeat on the other side. Transfer to a paper towel–lined plate

---

Recipe tip: Letting the vegetables sit after sprinkling them with salt helps draw out the moisture. This results in fritters that are nice and crispy instead of soggy.

Per serving: Total calories: 131; Total fat: 12g; Carbohydrates: 5g; Fiber: 1g; Sugars: 1g; Protein: 2g

PISTACHIO CRANBERRY ENERGY BITES

VEGETARIAN, DAIRY-FREE, SOY-FREE

Makes 10 to 12 balls :: Prep time: 15 minutes

These tasty snacks are loaded with protein and fiber. A perfect snack to take anywhere, they're especially great to munch on after exercising.

8 ounces (about 1 cup) dates, chopped

½ cup honey

1 tablespoon chia seeds

1 tablespoon ground flax seed

Pinch salt

1½ cups gluten-free old-fashioned oats

1 cup dried cranberries

1 cup shelled pistachios

⅓ cup chocolate chips

1. Combine the dates, honey, chia seeds, flax seeds, and salt in a blender or food processor and pulse until combined.
2. Transfer the mixture to a large bowl and stir in the oats, cranberries, pistachios, and chocolate chips.
3. Form into golf ball–size balls and store in the refrigerator until ready to eat.

Recipe tip: For perfectly round, uniform energy bites, use a small ice cream scoop to form the mixture into balls.

Per serving (1 ball): Total calories: 299; Total fat: 9g; Carbohydrates: 54g; Fiber: 5g; Sugars: 38g; Protein: 5g

SPICY AVOCADO DIP

VEGAN, DAIRY-FREE, NUT-FREE, SOY-FREE

Serves 4 :: Prep time: 10 minutes

Think of this dip as guacamole's kicky cousin. Avocados are a nutrient-dense food, featuring nearly 20 vitamins and minerals. They contain heart-healthy monounsaturated fat, also called "good fat."

2 large, ripe avocados

2 garlic cloves, crushed

Juice of 1 lime

1 teaspoon chili powder, plus more for serving

Pinch salt

Freshly ground black pepper

1. Place the avocados, garlic, lime juice, and chili powder in a food processor and blend until smooth, about 1 minute. Season with salt, pepper, and additional chili powder, if desired.
2. Transfer to a bowl and garnish with the chili powder. Serve with your favorite gluten-free chips or alongside tacos.

Recipe tip: If you don't have a food processor, you can make this dip using a handheld potato masher, or even a fork. It might not be as creamy, but it will still taste great.

Per serving: Total calories: 168; Total fat: 15g; Carbohydrates: 9g; Fiber: 7g; Sugars: 1g; Protein: 2g

SWEET-AND-SOUR ZUCCHINI

VEGAN, DAIRY-FREE

Serves 4 :: Prep time: 15 minutes :: Cook time: 5 minutes

Tangy and delicious, this is a great side dish. Consider pairing this tasty zucchini with Fast Chicken Fried Rice (page 96).

2 large zucchini, thinly sliced into rounds

1 teaspoon salt

2 tablespoons peanut oil

½ to 1 red chile (depending on your spice tolerance), seeded and sliced into thin strips

1 garlic clove, thinly sliced

½ teaspoon fresh ginger, minced

1 tablespoon rice vinegar

1 tablespoon tamari or gluten-free soy sauce

2 teaspoons sugar

½ teaspoon sesame oil

2 scallions, thinly sliced

1 teaspoon toasted sesame seeds

1. Place the zucchini in a large colander, sprinkle with the salt, and cover with a small plate to weigh it down. Let stand for 15 minutes to let moisture out. Quickly rinse the zucchini in cold water. Transfer them to a plate with several paper towels to absorb more moisture.
2. Heat a wok over high heat and add the peanut oil, chile, garlic, and ginger. Sauté for a few seconds.
3. Stir in the zucchini and then add the vinegar, tamari, sugar, and sesame oil. Cook, stirring, for 2 minutes. Add the scallions and cook for 30 seconds.
4. Garnish with the sesame seeds and serve.

Recipe tip: Standard soy sauce contains gluten, but tamari (which tastes very similar) is a great gluten-free alternative. You can find tamari next to the soy sauce in your grocery store. If you're allergic to soy, coconut aminos has a similar flavor.

Per serving: Total calories: 108; Total fat: 8g; Carbohydrates: 9g; Fiber: 2g; Sugars: 5g; Protein: 3g

NO-BAKE PROTEIN ENERGY BALLS

VEGETARIAN, DAIRY-FREE, SOY-FREE

Makes 10 to 12 balls :: Prep time: 30 minutes

These sweet treats make for a great snack or even a breakfast on the go. They're packed with protein, making them a tasty and healthy hit.

- 2 cups gluten-free old-fashioned oats
- 1 cup natural peanut butter
- ¾ cup honey
- ½ cup chocolate protein powder
- ⅓ cup chocolate chips
- ⅓ cup toasted coconut flakes
- ¼ cup sliced almonds
- 1 tablespoon unsweetened cocoa powder
- 2 teaspoons vanilla extract

1. In a large bowl, combine all the ingredients and stir to incorporate.
2. Line a baking sheet with wax paper.
3. Roll the mixture into golf ball–size balls and place them on the prepared pan. Place in the refrigerator to chill for about 30 minutes. Once chilled, transfer them to a resealable bag and store them in the refrigerator until you're ready to eat them.

Recipe tip: If you have a peanut allergy, you can use almond butter instead of peanut butter.

Per serving (1 ball): Total calories: 383; Total fat: 20g; Carbohydrates: 43g; Fiber: 4g; Sugars: 29g; Protein: 15g

APPLE SANDWICHES WITH ALMOND BUTTER, CHOCOLATE CHIPS, AND GRANOLA

VEGAN, DAIRY-FREE, SOY-FREE

Serves 4 :: Prep time: 5 minutes

These sweet little sandwiches are a deceptively healthy snack. Almonds are a great source of omega-3 fatty acids that may help reduce the risk of heart disease. They're also loaded with unsaturated fats.

2 Granny Smith apples

2 red apples (any kind)

¾ cup almond butter

½ cup chocolate chips

⅓ cup gluten-free granola

1. Wash the apples and then pat them dry. Remove the cores and slice into ⅓-inch-thick rounds.
2. Spread almond butter on half of the apple slices, sprinkle with the chocolate chips and granola, and top with the remaining apple slices to resemble sandwiches.

Recipe tip: Use an apple corer to speed up your prep time. Also, if you don't have almond butter, peanut butter works, too.

Per serving: Total calories: 529; Total fat: 37g; Carbohydrates: 51g; Fiber: 8g; Sugars: 34g; Protein: 10g

ZUCCHINI PIZZA BITES

NUT-FREE

Serves 4 :: Prep time: 10 minutes :: Cook time: 5 minutes

These quick mini zucchini pizza bites are perfectly flavorful, kid-friendly, low-carb snacks.

2 large zucchini, cut into ¼-inch-thick rounds

Kosher salt

Freshly ground black pepper

Nonstick cooking spray

½ cup pizza sauce

¼ cup mini pepperoni slices

½ cup shredded mozzarella cheese

1 teaspoon Italian Seasoning (page 132)

1. Sprinkle salt and pepper over the zucchini rounds.
2. Line a baking pan with parchment paper and turn on the broiler.
3. Heat a grill pan over medium heat. Spray with the nonstick spray and grill the zucchini for about 2 minutes on each side.
4. Arrange the zucchini on the prepared baking pan. Top with the pizza sauce, pepperoni, cheese, and Italian seasoning. Broil for 1 to 2 minutes, watching carefully so they don't burn.

Per serving: Total calories: 122; Total fat: 7g; Carbohydrates: 10g; Fiber: 3g; Sugars: 5g; Protein: 8g

ROASTED CORN ON THE COB WITH PARMESAN CHEESE

VEGETARIAN, NUT-FREE, SOY-FREE

Serves 6 :: Prep time: 5 minutes :: Cook time: 25 minutes

Buttery and garlicky with a generous helping of Parmesan cheese, this riff on corn on the cob is a favorite in my house.

6 ears corn, in their husks

6 tablespoons butter, at room temperature

2 tablespoons chopped fresh parsley

2 garlic cloves, pressed

Kosher salt

Freshly ground black pepper

½ cup freshly grated Parmesan cheese

1. Preheat the oven to 375°F.
2. Trim the silk top of each ear of corn to prevent fire and burning.
3. Place the corn on a roasting pan and roast for about 25 minutes.
4. While the corn is roasting, combine the butter, parsley, and garlic in a small bowl. Season with salt and pepper.
5. Peel the corn and brush with the butter mixture.
6. Sprinkle the corn with the Parmesan cheese and serve.

Recipe tip: If you'd prefer not to roast the corn in the husks, simply shuck the corn and wrap the cobs in aluminum foil.

Per serving: Total calories: 265; Total fat: 16g; Carbohydrates: 28g; Fiber: 4g; Sugars: 9g; Protein: 8g

CHAPTER FIVE

VEGETARIAN AND VEGAN MAINS

Vegan Three-Bean Chili 54

Southern Rice and Beans 55

Mexican Chili Corn Pie 56

Tofu and Mixed Vegetable Stir-Fry 57

Soba Noodles with Mushrooms, Broccoli, and Tofu 58

Thai Stir-Fried Noodles with Roasted Peanuts 59

Veggie and Pineapple Fried Rice 60

Bean Burgers 61

Skillet Veggie Lasagna 62

Creamy Pasta with Spinach and Pecans 63

Margherita Pizza with Cauliflower Crust 64

Polenta with Sautéed Mushrooms 65

Mushroom Stroganoff 67

Orzo-Mushroom Pilaf 68

Vegetarian Casserole 69

< Thai Stir-Fried Noodles with Roasted Peanuts, page 59

VEGAN THREE-BEAN CHILI

VEGAN, DAIRY-FREE, NUT-FREE

Serves 6 :: Prep time: 10 minutes :: Cook time: 20 minutes

An inexpensive and easy to prepare dinner, this recipe is loaded with three kinds of beans that are all delicious, nutritious, and full of healthy fiber.

2 red bell peppers, halved lengthwise

3 tablespoons extra-virgin olive oil

1 cup onion, chopped

4 garlic cloves, thinly sliced

2 teaspoons ground cumin

1 teaspoon crushed red pepper

1 teaspoon paprika

¼ teaspoon salt

1 (28-ounce) can diced tomatoes

2 medium zucchini, cut into ½-inch cubes

2 cups vegetable broth

1 jalapeño, seeded and diced (optional)

1 (15-ounce) can black beans, rinsed and drained

1 (15-ounce) can cannellini beans, rinsed and drained

1 (15-ounce) can kidney beans, rinsed and drained

3 scallions, sliced

1. Preheat the broiler.
2. Place the bell peppers skin-side up on a foil-lined baking dish or sheet pan. Broil until blackened and blistered, 5 to 8 minutes. Remove the peppers from the oven, transfer to a bowl, cover with plastic wrap, and let them stand for 5 minutes. Remove the skins and chop the peppers.
3. Heat a Dutch oven over medium heat. Pour the oil into the pan, and then add the onion. Cook for 5 minutes, or until the onion is softened.
4. Stir in the garlic, cumin, crushed red pepper, paprika, and salt. Cook for 1 to 2 minutes, or until they become fragrant. Then add the roasted bell peppers, tomatoes and their juices, zucchini, broth, and jalapeño, (if using).
5. Bring to a simmer, stirring occasionally, and cook for 5 minutes. Add the beans and simmer for 3 minutes, stirring occasionally, until slightly thickened. Adjust the seasoning according to taste. Garnish with the scallions and serve.

Recipe tip: If you're not in a hurry, you can use dried beans instead of canned. Simply soak them overnight to remove their indigestible sugars.

Per serving: Total calories: 325; Total fat: 7g; Carbohydrates: 52g; Fiber: 13g; Sugars: 10g; Protein: 15g

SOUTHERN RICE AND BEANS

VEGAN, DAIRY-FREE, NUT-FREE, SOY-FREE

Serves 4 :: Prep time: 10 minutes :: Cook time: 20 minutes

These rice and beans are anything but simple. Layered with amazing flavors, this is delicious, filling Southern comfort food.

1 cup long-grain rice

2 tablespoons extra-virgin olive oil

1 onion, finely chopped

1 red bell pepper, chopped

1 green bell pepper, chopped

2 medium tomatoes, seeded and chopped

1 dried chipotle chile, finely chopped

1 cup canned red kidney beans, drained and rinsed

1 tablespoon fresh basil, chopped

2 teaspoons fresh thyme, chopped

1 teaspoon Homemade Cajun Seasoning (page 134)

Pinch salt

Freshly ground black pepper

Fresh basil leaves, for garnish

1. Cook the rice in lightly salted water for about 12 minutes. Transfer to a large bowl and set aside.
2. Heat the oil in a skillet. Add the onion and bell peppers and cook for 5 minutes until soft. Stir in the tomatoes and chile and cook for another 2 minutes.
3. Add the vegetable mixture and kidney beans to the cooked rice and gently combine.
4. Add the herbs and the Homemade Cajun Seasoning to the rice and stir to combine.
5. Season with salt and pepper, and garnish with fresh basil.

Per serving: Total calories: 330; Total fat: 8g; Carbohydrates: 57g; Fiber: 6g; Sugars: 5g; Protein: 9g

MEXICAN CHILI CORN PIE

VEGETARIAN

Serves 4 :: Prep time: 5 minutes :: Cook time: 25 minutes

This is a fun and tasty meal—a fiesta of flavors! Filled with kidney beans, corn, and tomatoes, it's also chock-full of fiber and vitamin C.

FOR THE FILLING

1 tablespoon canola oil

2 garlic cloves, crushed

1 red bell pepper, diced

1 celery stalk, chopped

2 cups diced canned tomatoes

1 (15¼-ounce) can corn, drained

1 cup canned kidney beans, drained and rinsed

1 teaspoon chili powder

2 tablespoons fresh cilantro, plus additional sprigs to garnish

Salt

Freshly ground black pepper

FOR THE TOPPING

⅔ cup cornmeal

1 tablespoon gluten-free all-purpose flour

2 teaspoons gluten-free baking powder

½ teaspoon salt

6 tablespoons milk

1 egg, beaten

1 tablespoon canola oil

1 cup grated Colby or Monterey Jack cheese

TO MAKE THE FILLING

1. Preheat the oven to 425°F.
2. While the oven is warming up, heat the oil in a large skillet and panfry the garlic, bell peppers, and celery for about 3 minutes, or until just softened.
3. Stir in the tomatoes, corn, beans, and chili powder, and season with salt and pepper. Bring to a boil, and then lower the heat to a simmer for 5 minutes. Stir in the cilantro and transfer to a 9-by-9-inch ovenproof baking dish.

TO MAKE THE TOPPING

4. For the topping, use a handheld mixer to combine the cornmeal, flour, baking powder, and salt in a medium bowl. Make a well in the middle, and then add the milk, egg, and oil. Mix until smooth.
5. Spoon the topping over the top of the baking dish. Sprinkle the cheese on top and bake for 15 to 25 minutes, or until golden brown.
6. Garnish with the cilantro sprigs and serve.

Per serving: Total calories: 426; Total fat: 16g; Carbohydrates: 52g; Fiber: 8g; Sugars: 10g; Protein: 18g

TOFU AND MIXED VEGETABLE STIR-FRY

VEGAN, DAIRY-FREE, NUT-FREE

Serves 4 :: Prep time: 15 minutes :: Cook time: 10 minutes

High in protein and essential amino acids that our bodies need, tofu is a staple of many vegetarian diets—though it's great for omnivores as well. Opt for the non-GMO organic brands for maximum health benefits.

⅓ cup water

3 tablespoons gluten-free soy sauce or tamari

3 tablespoons sweet chili sauce

1 teaspoon cornstarch

3 tablespoons vegetable oil, divided

8 ounces firm tofu, cut into cubes

2 garlic cloves, minced

1 small onion, sliced into thin wedges

2 medium carrots, chopped

1 red bell pepper, thinly sliced

5 ounces broccoli, broken into small florets

1 large zucchini, chopped

5 ounces snap peas

Fresh baby basil leaves, for garnish

1. In a small bowl, combine the water, soy sauce, chili sauce, and cornstarch.
2. Heat 1 tablespoon of oil in a wok until it starts to smoke, then add the tofu and stir-fry over high heat for 2 minutes until golden brown. Transfer the tofu to a plate and set aside.
3. Heat the remaining 2 tablespoons of oil in the wok, then add the garlic, onion, and carrots and cook for about 3 minutes. Add the bell pepper and broccoli and cook for another 2 minutes.
4. Stir in the zucchini and snap peas and cook for 1 minute.
5. Stir in the soy sauce mixture and tofu, and then cook for 1 minute. Garnish with the fresh baby basil leaves and serve.

Recipe tip: Want to know the secret to getting deliciously crispy tofu? After slicing and drying the tofu, lay it flat on a cutting board or sheet pan lined with paper towels, and press down with more paper towels to expel excess moisture. Then sprinkle the tofu with cornstarch and fry on high heat.

Per serving: Total calories: 221; Total fat: 13g; Carbohydrates: 20g; Fiber: 5g; Sugars: 9g; Protein: 10g

SOBA NOODLES WITH MUSHROOMS, BROCCOLI, AND TOFU

VEGAN, DAIRY-FREE, NUT-FREE

Serves 4 :: Prep time: 10 minutes :: Cook time: 15 minutes

Authentic soba noodles are made of buckwheat flour and are gluten-free. They're a great alternative to traditional noodles and pasta made from wheat flour. You can find them in the international foods aisle in your grocery store.

8 ounces soba noodles

2 teaspoons sesame oil

½ cup vegetable stock

4 tablespoons tamari or gluten-free soy sauce

1 tablespoon brown sugar

1 tablespoon canola oil

3 garlic cloves, minced

1 tablespoon fresh ginger, minced

6 ounces fresh shiitake mushrooms, stemmed and sliced

½ pound firm tofu, cut into cubes

1 bunch baby broccoli

1 bunch scallions cut into 1-inch pieces

⅓ cup fresh cilantro, chopped

Salt (optional)

1. Bring a pot of water to a boil and cook the soba noodles according to the package directions. Drain and toss with the sesame oil. Set aside.
2. In a bowl, combine the vegetable stock, tamari, and brown sugar.
3. Heat a wok over high heat. Add the canola oil, garlic, and ginger, and stir-fry for about 10 seconds.
4. Add the mushrooms and stir-fry for about 2 minutes. Add the tofu, broccoli, and scallions and cook for another 2 minutes.
5. Add the noodle-and-liquid mixture to the wok. Reduce the heat to medium and cook for 2 more minutes before adding the cilantro. Adjust the salt to taste and serve.

Recipe tip: Make sure to buy soba noodles made of 100 percent buckwheat only. Some brands add wheat flour to their products, which makes it unsafe for people with gluten sensitivities and celiac disease. Always check the labels to be safe.

Per serving: Total calories: 353; Total fat: 9g; Carbohydrates: 59g; Fiber: 3g; Sugars: 6g; Protein: 17g

THAI STIR-FRIED NOODLES WITH ROASTED PEANUTS

VEGAN, DAIRY-FREE

Serves 4 :: Prep time: 15 minutes :: Cook time: 10 minutes

Instead of ordering out from your local Thai food place, try this vegan alternative. The smoked bean curd makes an excellent substitute for chicken or shrimp. You'll be loving the money you save—and the taste.

- ½ pound dried rice noodles
- 2 tablespoons canola oil
- 6 ounces smoked bean curd, cut into ½-inch cubes
- 2 shallots, finely chopped
- 2 garlic cloves, minced
- 1 red bell pepper, finely chopped
- 1 green bell pepper, finely chopped
- 1 cup bean sprouts
- 2 tablespoons tamari or gluten-free soy sauce
- 1 teaspoon sesame oil
- 1 teaspoon vegan fish sauce
- Salt
- Freshly ground black pepper
- 2 tablespoons chopped roasted peanuts
- Lime wedges, for serving

1. Cook the rice noodles according to the package directions. Drain and set aside.
2. Heat a wok over medium-high heat and add the canola oil. Sauté the bean curd for 1 minute, and then transfer to a plate. Add the shallots and garlic to the wok and sauté for 30 seconds, then add the bell peppers. Cook for 5 minutes, or until slightly soft.
3. Stir in the noodles, bean curd, bean sprouts, tamari, sesame oil, and vegan fish sauce. Cook for another 2 to 3 minutes, stirring constantly. Season with salt and pepper.
4. Top with the roasted peanuts and serve with lime wedges.

Recipe tip: If you can't find vegan fish sauce, use extra gluten-free soy sauce or tamari with a splash of lime juice.

Per serving: Total calories: 394; Total fat: 15g; Carbohydrates: 52g; Fiber: 3g; Sugars: 5g; Protein: 14g

VEGGIE AND PINEAPPLE FRIED RICE

VEGETARIAN, DAIRY-FREE, NUT-FREE

Serves 4 :: Prep time: 10 minutes :: Cook time: 20 minutes

You'll swear that this fried rice is just like the kind you get from your favorite Chinese food place. Pineapple balances out the stronger garlic and onion flavors. The taste will make people think you spent much more time making it than you actually did.

2 cups uncooked white rice or 5 to 6 cups leftover rice

4 tablespoons butter, divided

1 medium onion, chopped

3 large carrots, peeled and chopped

4 small zucchini, chopped

Salt

Freshly ground black pepper

5 garlic cloves, minced

1 cup pineapple chunks

5 tablespoons tamari or gluten-free soy sauce

1 tablespoon sesame oil

1 bunch scallion, chopped, for garnish

1. Cook the rice according to the package directions.
2. Heat a large cast iron pan over medium heat. Add 2 tablespoons of butter and sauté the onion for 3 to 4 minutes, or until it starts to brown.
3. Add the carrots and cook for 2 minutes, then add the zucchini. Cook for 3 minutes, or until the vegetables are tender. Season with salt and pepper and set aside.
4. Heat a wok over medium heat and add the remaining 2 tablespoons of butter. Sauté the garlic for 1 minute.
5. Add the rice and pineapple to the wok. Using a metal spatula, make sure you get to the bottom of the pan and gently incorporate the rice and garlic.
6. Stir in the vegetable mixture, then add the tamari and sesame oil and cook for 3 more minutes. Season with salt and pepper, and garnish with the scallions before serving.

Recipe tip: You can add any vegetables you like to this dish, including green peas, snow peas, corn, or bell peppers.

Per serving: Total calories: 564; Total fat: 16g; Carbohydrates: 94g; Fiber: 6g; Sugars: 10g; Protein: 12g

BEAN BURGERS

VEGETARIAN

Makes 6 burgers :: Prep time: 15 minutes :: Cook time: 15 minutes

This vegetarian alternative to a juicy beef burger hits the spot. Great for a quick lunch or dinner, it's sure to be a hit with people of all ages.

1 tablespoon extra-virgin olive oil

½ medium yellow onion, coarsely chopped

½ bell pepper, coarsely chopped

2 whole garlic cloves, peeled

2 (14-ounce) cans black beans, rinsed, drained well, and patted dry, divided

½ cup gluten-free bread crumbs

½ cup feta cheese

2 eggs

2 tablespoons ketchup

1 tablespoon vegetarian or vegan gluten-free Worcestershire sauce

1 teaspoon chili powder

¼ teaspoon paprika

Salt

Freshly ground black pepper

Nonstick cooking spray

6 gluten-free hamburger buns

TOPPING OPTIONS

Lettuce, grilled red onions, cheese, tomato slices

1. Heat a skillet over medium heat. Add the oil and sauté the onion, bell pepper, and garlic for about 5 minutes. Remove from the pan and use a paper towel to blot the moisture.
2. Place the vegetable mixture in a food processor with 1 can of beans, the bread crumbs, feta cheese, eggs, ketchup, Worcestershire sauce, chili powder, and paprika. Season with salt and pepper. Pulse until well blended, then add the remaining can of beans and pulse one more time, leaving some larger chunks of beans.
3. Form 6 patties.
4. Use nonstick spray to coat a grill or grill pan. Cook the burgers over medium-high heat for 3 to 4 minutes per side. Serve on the buns with your favorite toppings.

Per serving (1 burger): Total calories: 441; Total fat: 12g; Carbohydrates: 68g; Fiber: 11g; Sugars: 7g; Protein: 18g

SKILLET VEGGIE LASAGNA

VEGETARIAN, NUT-FREE, SOY-FREE

Serves 4 :: Prep time: 10 minutes :: Cook time: 20 minutes

A kid-friendly recipe with classic flavors, this veggie-filled lasagna is cheesy, delicious, and a great go-to for dinner.

1 tablespoon extra-virgin olive oil

1 small yellow onion, chopped

3 garlic cloves, minced

1 red bell pepper, chopped

1 zucchini, chopped

¼ teaspoon dried oregano

¼ teaspoon dried basil

Pinch crushed red pepper flakes

8 uncooked gluten-free lasagna noodles

1 (24-ounce) jar pasta sauce or Fresh Roasted Tomato Sauce (page 136)

1 (15-ounce) can diced tomatoes

Salt

Freshly ground black pepper

8 ounces spinach

½ cup ricotta cheese

6 ounces fresh mozzarella, thinly sliced

¼ cup grated Parmesan

⅓ cup chopped fresh basil

1. In a large skillet, heat the oil over medium-high heat. Add the onion and garlic, and cook for about 3 minutes before adding the bell pepper. Cook for 3 more minutes until the vegetables are tender.
2. Add the zucchini, oregano, basil, and red pepper flakes. Cook for another 2 minutes.
3. Remove the skillet from the heat. Place the lasagna noodles on top of the vegetables (you can break the noodles if they are too big).
4. Pour the pasta sauce and tomatoes over the noodles, making sure the noodles are covered. Season with salt and pepper.
5. Reduce the heat to medium and cover the skillet. Cook for 15 to 20 minutes, until the noodles are al dente.
6. Add the spinach and ricotta cheese to the skillet, and top with the mozzarella slices. Cover and let the cheese melt and the spinach wilt, about 3 minutes.
7. Top with the Parmesan cheese and fresh basil.

Recipe tip: To save time, you can use jarred minced garlic instead of chopping fresh garlic. Another way to cut down cooking time is to precook the lasagna noodles.

Per serving: Total calories: 648; Total fat: 21g; Carbohydrates: 91g; Fiber: 10g; Sugars: 14g; Protein: 24g

CREAMY PASTA WITH SPINACH AND PECANS

VEGETARIAN, SOY-FREE

Serves 4 :: Prep time: 5 minutes :: Cook time: 15 minutes

The flavors of the cream cheese and feta cheese in this recipe complement each other, making it a creamier take on a typical pasta dish. The pecans give it a nutty crunch that is bound to please.

12 ounces gluten-free penne

2 cups frozen peas

⅔ cup cream cheese with garlic and herbs

1 (6-ounce) package baby spinach

1 cup toasted pecans, chopped

1 cup crumbled feta cheese

Salt

Freshly ground black pepper

1. Cook the pasta according to the package directions. Add the peas for the final 2 minutes. Drain and reserve ½ cup of liquid. Transfer the pasta and peas to a bowl and set aside.
2. Heat a large pan and add the reserved liquid and cream cheese. Stir until the cream cheese is smooth and melted, about 2 minutes.
3. Remove from heat, and add the pasta and peas, spinach, pecans, and feta cheese.
4. Season with salt and pepper, and toss together until the spinach has wilted.

Per serving: Total calories: 796; Total fat: 40g; Carbohydrates: 89g; Fiber: 13g; Sugars: 11g; Protein: 21g

MARGHERITA PIZZA WITH CAULIFLOWER CRUST

VEGETARIAN, NUT-FREE, SOY-FREE

Serves 2 :: Prep time: 5 minutes :: Cook time: 25 minutes

People are crazy about pizza with cauliflower crust. You have to try this easy recipe—not only is it a healthier version of a regular pizza, but it will definitely satisfy your pizza cravings.

2 cups grated cauliflower florets

1 cup shredded Parmesan cheese

1 large egg

½ cup pizza sauce, either your favorite jarred brand or Fresh Roasted Tomato Sauce (page 136)

2 medium tomatoes, thinly sliced

8 ounces buffalo mozzarella cheese, thinly sliced

Fresh basil leaves, for garnish

1. Preheat the oven to 400°F.
2. In a large pan, cook the cauliflower over medium heat for about 10 minutes. Keep the pan uncovered to allow the moisture let off from the cauliflower to evaporate.
3. Remove from heat. Let the cauliflower cool enough to handle before transferring to a mixing bowl. Mix in the Parmesan and egg and incorporate to form a ball.
4. Line a pizza pan with parchment paper and place the cauliflower mixture in the middle, pressing down gently to form a thin, flat pizza crust. Bake for 10 to 12 minutes.
5. Remove the pan from the oven and top the cauliflower crust with the pizza sauce, sliced tomatoes, and mozzarella. Return to the oven and cook for another 10 minutes, or until the cheese has melted. Garnish with the fresh basil leaves.

Recipe tip: This can also be made using Basic No-Knead Pizza Crust (page 140).

Per serving: Total calories: 642; Total fat: 42g; Carbohydrates: 19g; Fiber: 4g; Sugars: 10g; Protein: 49g

POLENTA WITH SAUTÉED MUSHROOMS

VEGETARIAN, NUT-FREE

Serves 4 :: Prep time: 10 minutes :: Cook time: 20 minutes

The mushrooms in this hearty dish give a wonderful counterpoint of flavors mixed with the Parmesan cheese and herbs. This can be a quick main course or a great addition to a vegetarian feast.

Nonstick cooking spray

4 cups salted water

Salt

1 cup instant polenta

4 tablespoons butter

½ cup grated Parmesan cheese, plus 3 tablespoons for garnish

Salt

Freshly ground black pepper

5 tablespoons extra-virgin olive oil, divided

1 pound baby bella mushrooms, cleaned and quartered

1 pound button or cremini mushrooms, trimmed and quartered

⅓ cup fresh parsley, chopped

1½ tablespoons fresh thyme, chopped

1 cup vegetable broth

1. Coat an 11-by-7-inch baking dish with nonstick spray.
2. In a large saucepan, bring the water to a boil. Very slowly add the polenta while whisking constantly to avoid clumping. Reduce the heat to medium, and continue to cook, whisking constantly for 3 minutes.
3. Stir in the butter and ½ cup of grated Parmesan. Season with salt and pepper.
4. Pour the polenta into the prepared baking dish. Let it cool in the refrigerator while you continue cooking.
5. In a large skillet, heat 3 tablespoons of oil over high heat. Add the mushrooms and stir occasionally for about 8 minutes, or until they turn golden brown and release their liquids.
6. Stir in the parsley and thyme and then add the broth. Scrape the brown bits off the bottom of the pan. Cook for about 4 minutes, or until the liquid has evaporated. Adjust the seasoning according to taste.

continued >

POLENTA WITH SAUTÉED MUSHROOMS

continued

7. Remove the polenta from the refrigerator. Loosen the polenta from the pan and transfer to a cutting board. Cut into 4 slices.
8. Heat the remaining 2 tablespoons of oil in a nonstick skillet over medium-high heat. Cook the polenta for about 3 minutes per side, or until golden brown. Add more oil as needed.
9. Spoon the sautéed mushrooms over each slice of polenta and serve.

Recipe tip: If you don't have any nonstick cooking spray, a teaspoon of olive oil can also be used to grease the baking pan.

Per serving: Total calories: 512; Total fat: 33g; Carbohydrates: 41g; Fiber: 5g; Sugars: 4g; Protein: 16g

MUSHROOM STROGANOFF

VEGETARIAN, NUT-FREE

Serves 4 :: Prep time: 10 minutes :: Cook time: 15 minutes

This vegetarian take on a meaty comfort food is a creamy delight.

8 ounces gluten-free pasta

2 tablespoons butter

1 onion, chopped

3 garlic cloves, minced

6 cups coarsely chopped white button mushrooms

1 tablespoon fresh thyme leaves

1 cup milk

1 cup vegetable broth

¼ cup gluten-free all-purpose flour

1 teaspoon salt

¼ teaspoon freshly ground black pepper

2 tablespoons chopped fresh parsley, for garnish

3 tablespoons grated Parmesan, for garnish

1. Cook the pasta according to the package directions.
2. Melt the butter in a large pan and sauté the onion and garlic for about 5 minutes. Add the mushrooms and cook for about 8 minutes, or until tender and browned. Sprinkle the thyme over the mushrooms.
3. While the mushrooms are cooking, whisk the milk, broth, flour, salt, and pepper in a bowl.
4. Add the broth mixture to the mushrooms and cook for 2 to 3 minutes, or until the mixture thickens. If the mixture is too thick, slowly add more broth until you reach the desired consistency.
5. Add the pasta and stir to combine. Garnish with the parsley and Parmesan cheese and serve.

Per serving: Total calories: 374; Total fat: 9g; Carbohydrates: 63g; Fiber: 7g; Sugars: 8g; Protein: 13g

ORZO-MUSHROOM PILAF

VEGETARIAN, NUT-FREE

Serves 4 :: Prep time: 5 minutes :: Cook time: 20 minutes

You could pair this dish with your favorite main protein or serve it as a stand-alone light dinner. Using orzo makes a nice break from the standard risotto dishes.

2 tablespoons extra-virgin olive oil

1 small yellow onion, chopped

8 ounces sliced white or brown mushrooms

1 large carrot, sliced into thin rounds

Salt

Freshly ground black pepper

2 garlic cloves, minced

⅔ cup gluten-free orzo

1 (14-ounce) can low-sodium vegetable broth

1 teaspoon chopped fresh rosemary

1 tablespoon chopped fresh parsley

Grated Parmesan, for garnish (optional)

1. Heat the oil in a large skillet. Add the onion, mushrooms, and carrots, and season with salt and pepper. Cook for 5 minutes, stirring occasionally.
2. Stir in the garlic and cook for 30 seconds.
3. Add the orzo, broth, and rosemary. Bring to a slow boil, then reduce the heat to a simmer and cover. Cook for about 10 minutes, stirring occasionally.
4. Remove from the heat and let stand covered for 5 minutes longer.
5. Stir in parsley and adjust seasoning. Serve with grated Parmesan cheese if desired.

Recipe tip: Wild rice is a good substitute for orzo. It might take a little longer to cook, but it is just as delicious.

Per serving: Total calories: 200; Total fat: 8g; Carbohydrates: 27g; Fiber: 3g; Sugars: 5g; Protein: 6g

VEGETARIAN CASSEROLE

VEGETARIAN, NUT-FREE

Serves 4 :: Prep time: 15 minutes :: Cook time: 10 minutes

The robust flavor profile of this casserole, along with the natural vitamins and proteins, makes this dish extra satisfying.

- 1½ pounds russet potatoes, peeled and sliced with a mandoline
- 5 tablespoons butter
- 2 tablespoons extra-virgin olive oil
- 1 red onion, cut into thin wedges
- 2 garlic cloves, crushed
- 2 large carrots, chopped
- 1 bunch broccoli, cut into small florets
- 8 ounces firm organic bean curd, cut into cubes
- Salt
- Freshly ground black pepper
- 2 tablespoons chopped fresh sage, divided
- 1 cup shredded cheese

1. Cook the sliced potatoes in a large pot of boiling water for 5 to 6 minutes. Carefully drain and set the potatoes aside.
2. Heat the butter and oil in a large ovenproof skillet. Sauté the onion and garlic together for about 3 minutes. Add the carrots and cook for another 2 minutes. Stir in the broccoli and bean curd and cook for 2 minutes more. Season with salt and pepper and transfer to a bowl.
3. In the same skillet, arrange half of the potatoes on the bottom of the pan.
4. Top with the cooked vegetables, and sprinkle 1 tablespoon of sage over the top.
5. Cover the vegetables with the remaining potatoes.
6. Preheat the broiler.
7. Sprinkle the cheese over the top of the casserole. Cover and cook for 3 to 5 minutes.
8. Remove the lid and transfer to the broiler. Broil until the cheese becomes slightly browned, about 2 minutes. Garnish with the remaining 1 tablespoon of sage and serve.

Recipe tip: If you don't have russet potatoes, Yukon Gold potatoes are good, too.

Per serving: Total calories: 534; Total fat: 33g; Carbohydrates: 46g; Fiber: 9g; Sugars: 7g; Protein: 20g

CHAPTER SIX

SEAFOOD MAINS

Braised Shrimp with Vegetables 72

Saucy Shrimp with Spaghetti 73

Shrimp and Pineapple Curry 74

Shrimp and Snow Pea Stir-Fry with Cashews 75

Pan-Fried Tilapia with Balsamic Cherry Tomatoes 76

Lime and Thyme Tuna Steaks 77

Blackened Salmon with Tomato Salsa 78

Baked Salmon with Lemon Butter and Pineapple Salsa 79

Pecan-Crusted Salmon 80

Baked Salmon with Tomatoes and Olives 81

< Baked Salmon with Lemon Butter and Pineapple Salsa, page 79

BRAISED SHRIMP WITH VEGETABLES

DAIRY-FREE, NUT-FREE

Serves 4 :: Prep time: 10 minutes :: Cook time: 15 minutes

My family loves shrimp. Delicately seasoned, this is a healthy dinner featuring lots of green vegetables. I think it's best served with white rice.

½ cup low-sodium chicken broth

1 teaspoon cornstarch

1 teaspoon oyster sauce

½ teaspoon grated fresh ginger

½ teaspoon salt

¼ teaspoon freshly ground black pepper

2 tablespoons vegetable oil, divided

1 pound large shrimp, shelled and deveined

8 ounces button mushrooms, cleaned and sliced

2 cups broccoli florets

1 (8-ounce) can bamboo shoots, drained and rinsed

6 ounces snap peas

1. In a small bowl, whisk together the broth, cornstarch, oyster sauce, ginger, salt, and pepper.
2. Heat 1 tablespoon of oil in a wok over high heat, and stir-fry the shrimp until they turn pink, about 3 minutes. Transfer to a plate and set aside.
3. Add the remaining 1 tablespoon of oil to the pan and stir-fry the mushrooms for 3 minutes.
4. Add the broccoli, bamboo shoots, and snap peas to the pan and cook for 2 more minutes.
5. Return the shrimp to the pan and stir in the sauce, heating until the sauce thickens.

Recipe tip: If you're a pescatarian, swap out the chicken broth for seafood stock. You can find it in the soup aisle at your local grocery store.

Per serving: Total calories: 255; Total fat: 10g; Carbohydrates: 10g; Fiber: 4g; Sugars: 5g; Protein: 32g

SAUCY SHRIMP WITH SPAGHETTI

NUT-FREE, SOY-FREE

Serves 6 :: Prep time: 15 minutes :: Cook time: 15 minutes

This mouthwatering shrimp and pasta recipe is another favorite of mine. The shallot flavor is complemented by basil and tomatoes to blend into a nice sauce for the pasta.

1 pound shrimp, shelled and deveined

Salt

Freshly ground black pepper

1½ packages (12-ounce) gluten-free spaghetti pasta

3 tablespoons butter

2 tablespoons extra-virgin olive oil

2 large shallots, finely chopped

2 garlic cloves, minced

Pinch red pepper flakes

1 cup cherry tomatoes, halved

1 (14.5-ounce) can chopped tomatoes with basil, garlic, and oregano

¼ cup chopped fresh basil

½ cup grated Parmesan cheese

2 tablespoons chopped fresh parsley, for garnish

1. Season the shrimp with salt and pepper.
2. Cook the spaghetti according to the package directions. Drain and set aside.
3. While the spaghetti is cooking, heat a large skillet over medium heat and add the butter and oil. Sauté the shallots, garlic, and red pepper flakes for about 2 minutes, then add the shrimp. Cook the shrimp for 3 to 5 minutes, or until they turn pink.
4. Transfer the shrimp to a plate and set aside.
5. Sauté the cherry tomatoes in the same skillet for about 3 minutes, then add the chopped tomatoes and basil. Simmer for 2 more minutes. Season with salt and pepper.
6. Stir in the spaghetti, shrimp, and Parmesan cheese. Garnish with the parsley and serve.

Recipe tip: If you can't find shallots, feel free to substitute ½ cup of chopped leeks or yellow onion. Red or white onions might be too powerful, but leeks and yellow onions have a mellower flavor.

Per serving: Total calories: 450; Total fat: 15g; Carbohydrates: 52g; Fiber: 2g; Sugars: 4g; Protein: 28g

SHRIMP AND PINEAPPLE CURRY

DAIRY-FREE, NUT-FREE

Serves 4 :: Prep time: 10 minutes :: Cook time: 15 minutes

This is not your typical curry—the flavors are so decadent. You can find curry paste, fish sauce, and coconut cream in the international food aisle of your local grocery store.

- 1½ cups uncooked white rice
- 1 tablespoon vegetable oil
- 1 pound jumbo shrimp, shelled and deveined
- 2 garlic cloves, thinly sliced
- 1½ cups fresh pineapple, chopped
- 1 cup coconut cream
- 2 tablespoons red curry paste
- 2 teaspoons fish sauce
- 2 teaspoons sugar
- Salt
- 2 tablespoons chopped fresh cilantro, for garnish

1. Prepare the rice according to the package directions.
2. While rice is cooking, heat the oil in a wok and sauté the shrimp and garlic. Cook for 3 to 5 minutes, or until the shrimp becomes pink, and transfer to a bowl.
3. In the same wok, add the pineapple, coconut cream, curry paste, fish sauce, and sugar. Bring to a boil. Return the shrimp to the wok and add salt to taste.
4. Garnish with the fresh cilantro and serve with the rice.

Recipe tip: Fish sauce is a liquid condiment made from fermented fish. It has a very strong smell and taste. A good substitute for fish sauce is equal parts gluten-free soy sauce or tamari and lime juice.

Per serving: Total calories: 607; Total fat: 21g; Carbohydrates: 67g; Fiber: 2g; Sugars: 8g; Protein: 34g

SHRIMP AND SNOW PEA STIR-FRY WITH CASHEWS

DAIRY-FREE

Serves 4 :: Prep time: 10 minutes :: Cook time: 15 minutes

This dish is so easy to make and beats any Chinese takeout, at least in my neighborhood. The snow peas and cashews add a crunchy texture to the whole dish.

¼ cup low-sodium chicken broth

3 tablespoons gluten-free soy sauce or tamari

1 teaspoon cornstarch

3 tablespoons peanut oil

2 garlic cloves, thinly sliced

2 celery stalks, chopped

1 medium carrot, peeled and cut into matchsticks

6 ounces sliced white button mushrooms

1 pound large shrimp, shelled and deveined

2 cups shredded Chinese cabbage

6 ounces snow peas, ends trimmed

4 scallions, chopped

½ cup toasted cashews

1. In a small bowl, whisk the broth, soy sauce, and cornstarch. Set aside.
2. Heat a wok over medium-high heat and add the peanut oil. Sauté the garlic for about 1 minute, or until fragrant.
3. Add the celery, carrots, and mushrooms and cook for 3 minutes.
4. Add the shrimp, cabbage, snow peas, and scallions. Cook for 3 to 5 minutes, or until the shrimp become pink.
5. Stir in the cornstarch mixture. Cook for about 2 minutes, or until slightly thickened.
6. Top with the cashews and serve.

Recipe tip: Chinese cabbage, also known as Napa cabbage, is sweeter and softer than green cabbage.

Per serving: Total calories: 366; Total fat: 20g; Carbohydrates: 14g; Fiber: 3g; Sugars: 4g; Protein: 35g

PAN-FRIED TILAPIA WITH BALSAMIC CHERRY TOMATOES

Serves 4 :: Prep time: 10 minutes :: Cook time: 20 minutes

If someone in your house is fish-phobic, you can ease them into the seafood world with tilapia. Tilapia is a mild fish that pairs well with a variety of flavors. One of my favorite things to pair with it is this fresh, balsamic cherry tomato sauce with salty capers.

4 tilapia fillets

Salt

Freshly ground black pepper

½ cup gluten-free all-purpose flour

4 tablespoons butter

2 garlic cloves, minced

2 cups cherry tomatoes, quartered

1 cup low-sodium chicken broth

2 tablespoons capers

2 tablespoons balsamic vinegar

1. Dry the tilapia fillets with paper towels. Season with salt and pepper.
2. Place the flour in a shallow dish. Lightly coat the fish with the flour on both sides, shaking off any excess.
3. Melt the butter in a pan over medium-high heat. When hot, add the tilapia, cooking 2 to 3 minutes per side until nicely browned. Transfer to a platter.
4. Add the garlic to the same pan and sauté for 10 seconds, then add the tomatoes and cook for 3 minutes.
5. Stir in the broth, scraping the bottom to loosen any browned bits. Add the capers and balsamic vinegar and cook for 2 more minutes.
6. Top the fish with the tomato sauce and serve.

Recipe tip: Be sure to cook the fish in batches to avoid overcrowding in the pan.

Per serving: Total calories: 279; Total fat: 15g; Carbohydrates: 16g; Fiber: 3g; Sugars: 3g; Protein: 23g

LIME AND THYME TUNA STEAKS

DAIRY-FREE, NUT-FREE, SOY-FREE

Serves 4 :: Prep time: 10 minutes :: Cook time: 15 minutes

Tuna steaks have a firm, dense texture, kind of like a regular steak. This tuna recipe is accented with a delicate blend of lime and thyme that is so flavorful. This would go great with white rice and a simple green salad.

4 tuna steaks

3 tablespoons fresh thyme leaves

Zest of 2 limes

Salt

Freshly ground black pepper

3 tablespoons extra-virgin olive oil

Juice of 1 lime

1. Pat the tuna steaks dry with paper towels.
2. In a shallow bowl, mix the thyme and lime zest.
3. Season the tuna steaks with salt and pepper, and then rub them with the thyme mixture on both sides.
4. Heat the oil in a cast iron pan over medium-high heat. Sear the tuna for 1 to 2 minutes per side, depending on the steak's thickness and desired doneness.
5. Drizzle with lime juice just before serving.

Recipe tip: If you don't have a zester, you can use a fine cheese grater to zest the limes. Be careful not to grate past the colored part of the peel—the pith, or white part, is bitter.

Per serving: Total calories: 164; Total fat: 1g; Carbohydrates: 1g; Fiber: 1g; Sugars: <1g; Protein: 34g

BLACKENED SALMON WITH TOMATO SALSA

DAIRY-FREE, NUT-FREE, SOY-FREE

Serves 4 :: Prep time: 15 minutes :: Cook time: 15 minutes

This salmon, perfectly seasoned with Cajun spices, is a quick, tasty meal. The salmon's bold flavor holds its own against the punchy seasoning.

FOR THE SALSA

4 Roma tomatoes, seeded and chopped

¼ cup chopped red onion

3 tablespoons chopped fresh cilantro

2 tablespoons extra-virgin olive oil

1 small jalapeño pepper, minced

Juice of ½ lime

Salt

Freshly ground black pepper

FOR THE SALMON

4 (6-ounce) salmon fillets with skin

1 tablespoon Homemade Cajun Seasoning (page 134)

2 tablespoons extra-virgin olive oil

1. In a medium bowl, combine the salsa ingredients and set aside.
2. Sprinkle the salmon fillets with the Homemade Cajun Seasoning.
3. Heat a large skillet over medium heat and coat lightly with the oil.
4. Cook the salmon skin-side down for 2 to 3 minutes, then gently flip to cook the other side until crispy.
5. Cook for another 2 minutes, or until the fish looks blackened. Serve with the salsa.

Per serving: Total calories: 374; Total fat: 22g; Carbohydrates: 9g; Fiber: 2g; Sugars: 7g; Protein: 36g

BAKED SALMON WITH LEMON BUTTER AND PINEAPPLE SALSA

NUT-FREE

Serves 4 :: Prep time: 10 minutes :: Cook time: 20 minutes

Friends and family will love this salmon dish—especially the colorful pineapple salsa. It adds tart sweetness that complements the subtle flavor of the salmon. The lemon butter adds more flavor to the mix of the salsa and fish.

FOR THE LEMON BUTTER

2 tablespoons butter, softened

2 tablespoons lemon juice

1 tablespoon lemon zest

FOR THE SALSA

2 cups chopped fresh pineapple, chopped

¼ cup finely chopped fresh cilantro

3 tablespoons finely chopped red onion

Salt

Freshly ground black pepper

FOR THE SALMON

1 teaspoon extra-virgin olive oil or nonstick cooking spray

4 salmon fillets (about 1-inch thick)

Salt

Freshly ground black pepper

1. Preheat the oven to 375°F.
2. Mix the lemon butter ingredients in a small bowl. Set aside.
3. In another bowl, mix the salsa ingredients, and season with salt and pepper to taste. Cover and refrigerate the salsa while you cook the fish.
4. Grease a baking pan with the oil. Season the salmon with salt and pepper. Arrange the salmon on the prepared pan. Bake for 10 to 12 minutes, or until the fish flakes easily.
5. Top the fish with the lemon butter and salsa and serve.

Recipe tip: I used mango instead of pineapple once, and it was a hit with my family.

Per serving: Total calories: 315; Total fat: 14g; Carbohydrates: 11g; Fiber: 1g; Sugars: 8g; Protein: 35g

PECAN-CRUSTED SALMON

SOY-FREE

Serves 4 :: Prep time: 5 minutes :: Cook time: 15 minutes

Impress your family and friends with this pecan-crusted salmon. Moist inside and crunchy outside, this is best paired with roasted veggies or your favorite salad on the side.

1 teaspoon butter, plus 2 tablespoons, melted

4 salmon fillets (about 1½-inch thick) with skin

Salt

Freshly ground black pepper

2 tablespoons Dijon mustard

1½ tablespoons honey

¼ cup finely chopped pecans

¼ cup gluten-free bread crumbs

1 tablespoon chopped fresh parsley

Lemon wedges, for garnish

1. Preheat the oven to 450°F and grease a baking dish with 1 teaspoon of butter.
2. Season the fish with salt and pepper and place the fish skin-side down on the prepared pan.
3. In a small bowl, combine 2 tablespoons of butter, the mustard, and honey and brush it over the salmon.
4. In another bowl, combine the pecans, bread crumbs, and parsley. Spoon the mixture evenly over the top of the salmon fillets.
5. Bake for 12 to 15 minutes, or until the fish flakes easily. Garnish with the lemon wedges and serve.

Recipe tip: Cooking salmon with the skin on adds more flavor to the fish. Also, it makes it easier to separate the skin from the flesh if you don't like the way the skin tastes.

Per serving: Total calories: 373; Total fat: 19g; Carbohydrates: 12g; Fiber: 1g; Sugars: 7g; Protein: 36g

BAKED SALMON WITH TOMATOES AND OLIVES

DAIRY-FREE, NUT-FREE

Serves 4 :: Prep time: 5 minutes :: Cook time: 15 minutes

Add some zing to a salmon dinner with this delicious tomato sauce. The flavors of the thyme and vinegar blend wonderfully with the olives, capers, and tomatoes.

4 (6-ounce) salmon fillets

1 cup cherry tomatoes, halved

½ cup kalamata olives, pitted and chopped

2 tablespoons capers

3 thyme sprigs, plus a few more for garnish

3 tablespoons extra-virgin olive oil

2 tablespoons balsamic vinegar

Salt

Freshly ground black pepper

1. Preheat the oven to 400°F.
2. Arrange the salmon fillets in a baking dish and top with the tomatoes, olives, capers, and thyme sprigs.
3. Drizzle the oil and balsamic vinegar over the baking dish, and season with salt and pepper.
4. Bake for about 15 minutes. Garnish with the thyme sprigs before serving.

Recipe tip: You can also make this with ocean trout instead of salmon.

Per serving: Total calories: 357; Total fat: 21g; Carbohydrates: 5g; Fiber: 1g; Sugars: 2g; Protein: 35g

CHAPTER SEVEN

POULTRY MAINS

Chicken with Garlic, Bacon, and Thyme 84

Garlicky Broiled Chicken Thighs 85

Cheesy Chicken Wings 86

Sweet-and-Spicy Barbecue Chicken 87

Popcorn Chicken with Mashed Potatoes and Gravy 88

Chicken Tender Nachos 90

Sheet-Pan Chicken Fajitas 91

Pepper Jack–Stuffed Chicken 92

Asian Chicken Lettuce Wraps 93

Grilled Chicken with Pineapple-Ginger Glaze 94

Sweet-and-Sour Chicken Stir-Fry 95

Fast Chicken Fried Rice 96

Teriyaki Chicken Burgers 97

Turkey Cutlets with Pepper and Tomato Ragout 98

Turkey Meat Loaf 99

< Sheet-Pan Chicken Fajitas, page 91

CHICKEN WITH GARLIC, BACON, AND THYME

Serves 4 :: Prep time: 10 minutes :: Cook time: 20 minutes

You simply can't go wrong with bacon, butter, garlic, and fresh herbs. This dish features all of the above. Paired with boneless chicken breasts, this classic combo is perfect for any day of the week.

4 boneless chicken breasts, halved

½ teaspoon salt

¼ teaspoon freshly ground black pepper

¼ cup gluten-free all-purpose flour

6 strips bacon, chopped

1 tablespoon butter

2 garlic cloves, thinly sliced

1 tablespoon minced fresh thyme

Pinch crushed red pepper flakes

1 cup low-sodium chicken broth

2 tablespoons lemon juice

1. Pound chicken breasts slightly with a meat mallet for uniform thickness. Season with the salt and pepper.
2. Place the flour in a shallow bowl. Dip the chicken in the flour, shake off the excess, and set the chicken aside.
3. Cook the bacon in a large skillet over medium heat until crispy, stirring occasionally. Remove with a slotted spoon onto a paper towel–lined plate. Reserve about 3 tablespoons of bacon drippings in the pan, discarding the rest.
4. Add the butter to the skillet. Let it melt, then add the chicken and cook for 4 minutes per side, in batches, until cooked through. Transfer the chicken to a paper towel–lined plate.
5. In the same skillet, add the garlic, thyme, and red pepper flakes. Cook, stirring, for 1 minute. Add the broth and lemon juice. Bring to a slow boil until the liquid is reduced by half. Return the bacon and chicken to the pan and heat through before serving.

Recipe tip: If you don't have a meat mallet, you can use a rolling pin or even a heavy frying pan to pound the chicken breasts.

Per serving: Total calories: 234; Total fat: 10g; Carbohydrates: 7g; Fiber: 1g; Sugars: <1g; Protein: 30g

GARLICKY BROILED CHICKEN THIGHS

NUT-FREE

Serves 4 :: Prep time: 5 minutes :: Cook time: 20 minutes

When you want something crispy and garlicky, this will satisfy your cravings. Remember, gluten-free doesn't have to mean bland. These delicious chicken thighs are crunchy and flavorful.

- 8 bone-in chicken thighs
- ⅓ cup butter
- ¼ cup tamari or gluten-free soy sauce
- 6 garlic cloves, minced
- ½ teaspoon freshly ground black pepper

1. Preheat the oven to broil.
2. Place the chicken thighs in a large bowl and pat them dry with paper towels.
3. In another bowl, whisk together the butter, tamari, garlic, and pepper. Reserve about ¼ cup of the sauce mixture for basting, and pour the remaining sauce mixture over chicken and toss to coat. Let it sit for a few minutes.
4. Place chicken skin-side down on a sheet pan. Broil about 5 to 6 inches from the heat for 10 to 15 minutes.
5. Flip chicken and broil for another 10 minutes, brushing occasionally with the reserved sauce, until an instant thermometer inserted in the chicken reads 175°F.

Recipe tip: **Keep an eye on the chicken while it is cooking. If you're not careful, broiling can burn meat and vegetables fast.**

Per serving: Total calories: 628; Total fat: 49g; Carbohydrates: 2g; Fiber: <1g; Sugars: <1g; Protein: 40g

CHEESY CHICKEN WINGS

NUT-FREE, SOY-FREE

Serves 4 :: Prep time: 5 minutes :: Cook time: 25 minutes

These cheesy wings make a scrumptious supper and are great for feeding a crowd, especially during football season. Pair them with your favorite salad or corn on the cob for a complete dinner experience.

- 6 tablespoons melted butter, plus 1 teaspoon butter, divided
- 1 cup gluten-free bread crumbs
- 1 cup grated Parmesan cheese
- 1½ teaspoons dried basil leaves
- 1 teaspoon dried oregano
- 1 teaspoon garlic salt
- 5 pounds plain (about 35) chicken wings

1. Preheat the oven to 375°F and lightly grease a large baking pan with 1 teaspoon of butter.
2. In a bowl, combine the Parmesan cheese, bread crumbs, basil, oregano, and garlic salt.
3. Place 6 tablespoons of melted butter in a bowl. Dip the chicken wings first into the butter and then into the bread crumb mixture. Arrange the wings in the prepared pan.
4. Bake chicken wings for about 25 minutes, or until lightly browned and tender.

Recipe tip: You can find grated or crumbled Parmesan cheese pretty easily in the grocery store, but I think freshly grating your own tastes best.

Per serving: Total calories: 803; Total fat: 66g; Carbohydrates: 20g; Fiber: 1g; Sugars: 1g; Protein: 61g

SWEET-AND-SPICY BARBECUE CHICKEN

NUT-FREE

Serves 4 :: Prep time: 10 minutes :: Cook time: 20 minutes

This dish is perfect for a summer party. The kick of spice from the chili powder, garlic, and cumin and the sweetness of the barbecue sauce make this dish perfectly balanced.

1 teaspoon garlic powder

1 teaspoon chili powder

½ teaspoon ground cumin

½ teaspoon paprika

½ teaspoon crushed red pepper flakes

½ teaspoon salt

4 boneless, skinless chicken thighs

¼ cup gluten-free barbecue sauce (either store-bought or Barbecue Sauce, page 139)

¼ cup honey

1. Preheat a gas grill to high heat.
2. Combine the garlic powder, chili powder, cumin, paprika, red pepper flakes, and salt, and rub the mix over the chicken pieces.
3. Grill the chicken for 3 to 5 minutes per side.
4. In a separate bowl, mix the barbecue sauce and honey.
5. Lower the heat on the grill to medium and brush the chicken with the barbecue sauce mixture. Continue to grill the chicken until cooked through and the internal temperature reaches 165°F.

Recipe tip: If you don't feel like grilling (or the weather isn't cooperating), simply bake the chicken at 400°F for 25 to 30 minutes. Baste with the barbecue sauce and broil for an additional 3 minutes. You can also make this on a charcoal grill if you are not pressed for time.

Per serving: Total calories: 212; Total fat: 7g; Carbohydrates: 21g; Fiber: 1g; Sugars: 23g; Protein: 17g

POPCORN CHICKEN WITH MASHED POTATOES AND GRAVY

NUT-FREE

Serves 4 :: Prep time: 10 minutes :: Cook time: 20 minutes

This delicious meal is one of my absolute favorites. The soft mashed potatoes go great with the crispy chicken, and everyone knows mashed potatoes and gravy are a match made in heaven.

FOR THE MASHED POTATOES

7 medium Yukon gold potatoes, peeled and cut into 1-inch cubes

½ cup milk

3 tablespoons butter

Salt

Freshly ground black pepper

FOR THE POPCORN CHICKEN

Cooking oil, such as vegetable or canola

1 cup gluten-free Italian bread crumbs

2 tablespoons cornstarch

1 teaspoon paprika

½ teaspoon chili powder

2 eggs

1 pound chicken tenderloin, cut into ½-inch pieces

FOR THE GRAVY

1 package gluten-free gravy mix

1 cup cold water

TO MAKE THE MASHED POTATOES

1. Place the potatoes in a large bowl with enough water and microwave for 8 to 10 minutes, or until tender.
2. Drain the potatoes, and then add the milk and butter. Use a potato masher and mash until soft, then season with salt and pepper.

TO MAKE THE POPCORN CHICKEN

3. While the potatoes are cooking, heat the oil in a deep fryer until the temperature reaches 350°F.
4. On a plate, mix the bread crumbs, cornstarch, paprika, and chili powder.
5. In a shallow bowl, beat the eggs. Dip a handful of chicken pieces into the eggs and then into the bread crumb mixture.
6. Fry the chicken in batches until crispy, about 3 minutes. Remove the chicken with a slotted spatula and place it on a paper towel–lined plate to remove excess oil.

TO MAKE THE GRAVY

In a small saucepan, combine the water and gravy mix. Cook over medium heat for about 2 minutes, stirring constantly until thickened.

TO SERVE

Scoop mashed potatoes onto a plate, top with the crispy popcorn chicken, and drizzle gravy over the top.

Per serving: Total calories: 580; Total fat: 15g; Carbohydrates: 76g; Fiber: 5g; Sugars: 5g; Protein: 37g

CHICKEN TENDER NACHOS

NUT-FREE, SOY-FREE

Serves 4 :: Prep time: 10 minutes :: Cook time: 20 minutes

I love digging into a pile of nachos. Give me a plate of chips, veggies, and protein, top it with melted cheese, and I'm a happy camper. I think this cheesy, spicy dish is best shared with family or friends.

8 slices bacon

1½ teaspoon paprika

1 teaspoon cumin

½ teaspoon cayenne pepper

1 teaspoon chili powder

1 teaspoon garlic salt

Extra-virgin olive oil, for cooking

3 pounds chicken tenderloins

1½ cups shredded Mexican cheese blend

1 jalapeño, thinly sliced

3 scallions, chopped

1. Preheat the oven to 375°F.
2. Cook the bacon in a skillet until crispy. Chop into small pieces and set aside.
3. In a small bowl, combine the paprika, cumin, cayenne pepper, chili powder, and garlic salt.
4. Pat the chicken dry with paper towels.
5. Sprinkle the seasoning mixture over the chicken.
6. Heat a large cast iron pan over medium heat. Add a splash of oil and then cook the chicken in batches for about 3 minutes per side until cooked through.
7. Arrange the cooked chicken on a baking dish and sprinkle with the cheese and jalapeños.
8. Bake for 3 to 5 minutes, or until the cheese has melted. Sprinkle with the crispy bacon and scallions before serving.

Recipe tip: Chicken breasts can be used here instead of tenderloins. You will need to cut them into smaller pieces, similar to the size of chicken tenders.

Per serving: Total calories: 561; Total fat: 22g; Carbohydrates: 4g; Fiber: 1g; Sugars: <1g; Protein: 83g

SHEET-PAN CHICKEN FAJITAS

NUT-FREE, SOY-FREE

Serves 4 :: Prep time: 10 minutes :: Cook time: 20 minutes

This is a quick and easy dinner, bursting with the savory blend of spices and the smoky-sweetness of the roasted bell peppers.

1 teaspoon extra-virgin olive oil, plus 1 tablespoon

1 red bell pepper, thinly sliced

1 green bell pepper, thinly sliced

1 orange bell pepper, thinly sliced

1 red onion, sliced into thin wedges

4 boneless, skinless chicken breasts, cut into strips

2 garlic cloves, minced

1 package gluten-free fajita seasoning

Salt

For serving

Corn tortillas

Sliced avocado

Sour cream

Fresh cilantro, chopped

Lime wedges

1. Preheat the oven to 400°F.
2. Lightly grease a 17-by-12-inch baking sheet with 1 teaspoon of oil.
3. Spread the bell peppers and onion on the baking sheet. Top with the chicken strips, sprinkle the garlic and fajita seasoning all over, season with salt, and then drizzle with the remaining 1 tablespoon of oil and gently toss to coat.
4. Evenly spread the mixture over the pan. Roast from 18 to 20 minutes, tossing once halfway through, until the chicken is cooked through and the vegetables are tender.
5. Warm the tortillas according to the package directions and serve with the toppings of your choice.

Per serving: Total calories: 207; Total fat: 7g; Carbohydrates: 15g; Fiber: 2g; Sugars: 5g; Protein: 24g

PEPPER JACK–STUFFED CHICKEN

NUT-FREE

Serves 4 :: Prep time: 5 minutes :: Cook time: 25 minutes

These simple, cheese-filled chicken breasts are deliciously seasoned, moist, and satisfying. Pair this chicken with your favorite salad. It's perfect for a family supper!

1 teaspoon vegetable oil, plus 2 tablespoons

4 boneless, skinless chicken breasts

3 tablespoons gluten-free taco seasoning

4 ounces pepper jack cheese, thinly sliced into 4 strips

1. Preheat the oven to 375°F and grease a sheet pan with 1 teaspoon of oil.
2. Cut the chicken breasts down the middle to create a pouch. Season the chicken with the taco seasoning, making sure to season within the pouch.
3. Place a strip of cheese in each pouch, fold, and secure with a toothpick.
4. Heat the remaining 2 tablespoons of oil in a large skillet and brown the chicken on both sides. Remove the toothpick once one side has already browned.
5. Transfer to the prepared pan and bake uncovered for 25 minutes, or until cooked through.

Recipe tip: Add some veggies to this dish by topping the chicken with your favorite salsa.

Per serving: Total calories: 291; Total fat: 19g; Carbohydrates: 4g; Fiber: 0g; Sugars: 1g; Protein: 29g

ASIAN CHICKEN LETTUCE WRAPS

DAIRY-FREE, NUT-FREE

Serves 4 :: Prep time: 10 minutes :: Cook time: 20 minutes

Hoisin sauce, often used in Asian cooking, gives this dish a sweet and savory flavor.

1 pound ground chicken

1 tablespoon extra-virgin olive oil

1 onion, finely chopped

2 garlic cloves, minced

2 teaspoons fresh ginger, grated

¼ cup gluten-free hoisin sauce

2 tablespoons tamari or gluten-free soy sauce

1 tablespoon rice wine vinegar

Salt

Freshly ground black pepper

1 head Boston lettuce, leaves separated and cleaned

3 scallions, thinly sliced

1. Brown the chicken in a saucepan over medium-high heat, about 3 minutes. Drain and transfer to a plate.
2. In the same pan, heat the oil, then add the onion and garlic. Sauté for about 3 minutes, or until soft and translucent. Stir in the ginger and cook 1 minute more.
3. Return the chicken to the pan, and add the hoisin sauce, tamari, and vinegar. Season with salt and pepper.
4. Arrange lettuce leaves on a platter. Top the lettuce with the cooked chicken and garnish with the scallions.

Recipe tip: Gluten-free hoisin sauce can be found in the international foods aisle of your grocery store or near the soy sauce.

Per serving: Total calories: 297; Total fat: 16g; Carbohydrates: 14g; Fiber: 3g; Sugars: 6g; Protein: 23g

GRILLED CHICKEN WITH PINEAPPLE-GINGER GLAZE

DAIRY-FREE, NUT-FREE

Serves 4 :: Prep time: 10 minutes :: Cook time: 20 minutes

Grilling is one of the best ways to cook with very little fat. It's also quick and gives the meat a great smoky flavor. The ginger adds a nice snap to the sweetness of the pineapple.

1 peeled and cored pineapple

¼ cup canned pineapple juice

¼ cup brown sugar

¼ cup tamari or gluten-free soy sauce

2 tablespoons ketchup

2 teaspoons minced fresh ginger

2 garlic cloves, minced

1 teaspoon sesame oil

1 teaspoon sriracha

4 chicken boneless, skinless breasts, halved

Nonstick cooking spray

3 tablespoons chopped fresh cilantro, for garnish

1. Cut the pineapple into eight ½-inch rounds.
2. In a medium bowl, combine the pineapple juice, brown sugar, tamari, ketchup, ginger, garlic, sesame oil, and sriracha. Reserve ¼ cup for basting.
3. Place the chicken in a large bowl and pour the rest of the sriracha mixture over the chicken. Let it sit for 15 minutes.
4. Preheat the grill to medium-high heat.
5. Coat the grill with the nonstick cooking spray, and grill the chicken for 4 to 5 minutes per side depending on thickness. Baste the chicken with the reserved sriracha mixture while grilling.
6. Grill the pineapple slices, basting a few times with the sriracha mixture, and cook for about 2 minutes per side. Serve with the grilled chicken. Garnish with the cilantro.

Recipe tip: If the weather isn't grill-friendly where you are, this can be cooked indoors in a large grill pan.

Per serving: Total calories: 247; Total fat: 4g; Carbohydrates: 34g; Fiber: 2g; Sugars: 23g; Protein: 26g

SWEET-AND-SOUR CHICKEN STIR-FRY

DAIRY-FREE, NUT-FREE

Serves 4 :: Prep time: 10 minutes :: Cook time: 15 minutes

Sweet-and-sour cooking originated in China, and this fresh homemade take on takeout has all the elements you're looking for. Serve with steamed white rice to complete the meal.

2 tablespoons vegetable oil

2 garlic cloves, thinly sliced

½ teaspoon grated fresh ginger

1½ to 2 pounds chicken breast or tenderloins, cut into bite-size pieces

4 cups frozen stir-fry vegetables, thawed

1 cup gluten-free sweet-and-sour sauce

Salt

Freshly ground black pepper

1. Heat a wok over high heat and add the oil, garlic, and ginger. Sauté for 15 seconds and then add the chicken. Cook the chicken for about 5 minutes, or until cooked through.
2. Stir in the vegetables and then the sauce, and cook for about 5 minutes, or until tender. Season with salt and pepper, and serve.

Recipe tip: Fresh vegetables are also welcome in this recipe instead of frozen ones.

Per serving: Total calories: 387; Total fat: 11g; Carbohydrates: 37g; Fiber: 2g; Sugars: 25g; Protein: 36g

FAST CHICKEN FRIED RICE

NUT-FREE

Serves 6 :: Prep time: 10 minutes :: Cook time: 20 minutes

This is a great way to use leftover chicken! You can also use precooked rotisserie chicken, and using frozen vegetables helps cut down on chopping time.

2 cups uncooked jasmine rice

1 small onion, chopped

2 large carrots, peeled and chopped

4 tablespoons butter, divided

3 medium zucchini, chopped

Salt

Freshly ground black pepper

4 large eggs, beaten

3 garlic cloves, minced

2 cups precooked chicken, chopped

6 tablespoons tamari or gluten-free soy sauce

1. Cook the rice according to the package directions.
2. Heat a cast iron pan over medium heat and sauté the onions and carrots with 2 tablespoons of butter. Stir in the zucchini and cook for 2 more minutes. Season with salt and pepper and set aside.
3. Heat 1 tablespoon of butter in a wok, scramble the eggs, remove to a plate, and set aside.
4. Add the remaining 1 tablespoon of butter to the wok, sauté the garlic for 30 seconds, and then add the rice. Stir the rice and garlic and cook for 3 minutes before adding the carrot-and-zucchini mixture, the chicken, and the scrambled eggs. Combine and then add the tamari. Adjust the salt and pepper to taste.

Recipe tip: If you have leftover rice, it would be perfect in this recipe.

Per serving: Total calories: 443; Total fat: 15g; Carbohydrates: 53g; Fiber: 2g; Sugars: 4g; Protein: 25g

TERIYAKI CHICKEN BURGERS

DAIRY-FREE, NUT-FREE

Serves 4 :: Prep time: 10 minutes :: Cook time: 20 minutes

If you think chicken burgers are boring, prepare to be proven wrong. This recipe is full of delicious Asian-inspired flavors.

1½ pound lean ground chicken

½ cup gluten-free bread crumbs

2 tablespoons tamari or gluten-free soy sauce

2 scallions, chopped

2 garlic cloves, minced

1 tablespoon brown sugar

1 teaspoon grated fresh ginger

½ teaspoon sesame oil

Pinch salt

Pinch freshly ground black pepper

2 tablespoons vegetable oil

4 gluten-free burger buns

TOPPING OPTIONS

Pineapple slices

Lettuce

Sliced red onion

1. Preheat the grill to medium-high heat.
2. In a large bowl, combine all the ingredients except the vegetable oil and hamburger buns. Mix well and shape into 4 patties about ½- to ¾-inch thick.
3. Brush the grill with the vegetable oil and grill the chicken burgers for 3 to 5 minutes per side, or until cooked through.
4. Serve on the buns with your topping choices.

Recipe tip: The burgers can be cooked in a pan instead of grilled.

Per serving: Total calories: 436; Total fat: 17g; Carbohydrates: 48g; Fiber: 5g; Sugars: 7g; Protein: 28g

TURKEY CUTLETS WITH PEPPER AND TOMATO RAGOUT

DAIRY-FREE, NUT-FREE, SOY-FREE

Serves 4 :: Prep time: 15 minutes :: Cook time: 15 minutes

Sometimes the simplest recipes are the ones that taste the best. This is one of them.

4 cups cherry tomatoes

2 red or orange bell peppers, cut into ¾-inch pieces

1 cup chopped sweet onion

6 tablespoons extra-virgin olive oil, divided

Salt

Freshly ground black pepper

1½ tablespoons capers

1½ pounds turkey cutlets (about 8 to 10 pieces)

1. Preheat the broiler.
2. In a large bowl, combine the tomatoes, bell peppers, and onion. Drizzle with 2 tablespoons of oil and season with salt and pepper, tossing to coat.
3. Transfer the vegetables to a broiler pan and broil for 3 minutes. Stir gently and broil until the vegetables are tender, about 4 minutes.
4. Remove the vegetables from the oven and transfer to a bowl. Stir in the capers and set aside.
5. Season the turkey cutlets with salt and pepper.
6. Heat a large nonstick skillet over medium-high heat. Add a splash of oil and cook the turkey in batches for 2 to 3 minutes per side.
7. Transfer the turkey to a platter and serve with the cooked vegetables.

Per serving: Total calories: 303; Total fat: 8g; Carbohydrates: 14g; Fiber: 4g; Sugars: 7g; Protein: 44g

TURKEY MEAT LOAF

Serves 4 :: Prep time: 5 minutes :: Cook time: 25 minutes

The mushrooms add a lot of flavor and substance to this moist and tasty meat loaf. It's a good choice for those who want to cut down on their red meat consumption.

2 tablespoons extra-virgin olive oil

1 small onion, finely chopped

2 garlic cloves, minced

6 ounces white button mushrooms, finely chopped

1 tablespoon gluten-free Worcestershire sauce

½ cup ketchup, divided

½ teaspoon salt

½ teaspoon freshly ground black pepper

1½ pounds ground turkey

1 cup gluten-free bread crumbs

2 large eggs

⅓ cup milk

1. Heat a large skillet over medium heat. Add the oil, onion, and garlic, and sauté for about 5 minutes, or until soft. Stir in the mushrooms and cook for about 6 minutes, or until the mushrooms become browned. Add the Worcestershire sauce and ¼ cup of ketchup. Season with the salt and pepper and transfer to a plate.
2. In a large bowl, combine the ground turkey, bread crumbs, eggs, milk, and mushroom mixture. (Just a heads-up, this will be very wet. That's okay!)
3. In a baking pan, form 2 meat loaves side by side and top with the remaining ¼ cup of ketchup, spreading evenly.
4. Bake at 375°F for about 25 minutes, or until the meatloaves register 170°F.

Per serving: Total calories: 494; Total fat: 27g; Carbohydrates: 34g; Fiber: 2g; Sugars: 4g; Protein: 38g

CHAPTER EIGHT

MEAT MAINS

Grilled Lime and Chili Pork Chops 102

Pork and Pineapple Stir-Fry 103

Skillet Pork Chops with Smashed Potatoes 104

Grilled Pork Tenderloin with Fruit Salsa 105

Kielbasa, Potato, and Pepper Supper 106

Rosemary-Garlic and Citrus Marinated Grilled Lamb Chops 107

Herb-Crusted Racks of Lamb 108

Grilled Loaded Flank Steaks with Corn Salsa 109

Grilled Steaks with Mushroom Sauce 110

Pressure Cooker Beef Stew 112

Easy Sloppy Joes 113

Barbecue Meat Loaf 114

Hamburger with Mushroom and Fusilli Pasta 115

Teriyaki Beef with Rice Noodles 116

Szechuan Beef with Snow Peas 117

< Grilled Loaded Flank Steaks with Corn Salsa, page 109

GRILLED LIME AND CHILI PORK CHOPS

DAIRY-FREE, NUT-FREE

Serves 4 :: Prep time: 15 minutes :: Cook time: 15 minutes

A spicy, tangy take on pork. The cilantro adds a cooling herbal flavor to offset the garlic salt.

1 tablespoon lime juice

1 tablespoon canola oil

1 teaspoon chili powder

½ teaspoon garlic salt

⅛ teaspoon ground cayenne pepper

4 boneless pork loin chops, ¾-inch thick

3 tablespoons chopped fresh cilantro

Lime wedges, for serving

1. Heat the grill to medium-high heat.
2. Mix the lime juice, oil, chili powder, garlic salt, and cayenne pepper in a small bowl.
3. Rub the pork on both sides with the spice mixture.
4. Grill for 5 to 7 minutes, or until pork is cooked through and no longer pink in the middle.
5. Sprinkle with the cilantro and serve with lime wedges.

Per serving: Total calories: 175; Total fat: 9g; Carbohydrates: 1g; Fiber: <1g; Sugars: <1g; Protein: 21g

PORK AND PINEAPPLE STIR-FRY

DAIRY-FREE, NUT-FREE

Serves 4 :: Prep time: 10 minutes :: Cook time: 20 minutes

You'll be surprised at how quickly this dish comes together for an easy meal. Prepackaged bags of veggies make it superfast if you don't have a lot of time to prep.

1 (20-ounce) can pineapple chunks
1 pound boneless lean pork, cut into thin strips
Salt
Freshly ground black pepper
⅓ cup water
3 tablespoons tamari or gluten-free soy sauce
1½ teaspoon cornstarch
½ teaspoon fresh ginger, grated
Pinch crushed red pepper flakes
3 tablespoons packed brown sugar, divided
1 tablespoon canola oil
1 (16-ounce) bag coleslaw mix (carrots and shredded cabbage)

1. Strain the canned pineapple, reserving 3 tablespoons of juice.
2. Season the pork with salt and pepper.
3. In a small bowl, combine the water, 2 tablespoons of brown sugar, the reserved pineapple juice, tamari, cornstarch, red pepper flakes, and set side.
4. Heat a nonstick skillet over medium-high heat. Add the pineapple chunks and sprinkle them with the remaining 1 tablespoon of brown sugar. Cook for 3 minutes, stirring occasionally. Transfer the pineapple to a plate.
5. In the same skillet, add the oil and stir-fry the pork, about 3 minutes.
6. Add the coleslaw mix, and stir and cook for another 3 minutes. Stir in the pineapple-and-cornstarch mixture. Cook until the sauce is slightly thickened. Serve with your favorite side dish.

Recipe tip: Other veggies such as broccoli, carrots, and green beans would also be good in this stir-fry.

Per serving: Total calories: 365; Total fat: 12g; Carbohydrates: 45g; Fiber: 4g; Sugars: 34g; Protein: 25g

SKILLET PORK CHOPS WITH SMASHED POTATOES

NUT-FREE

Serves 4 :: Prep time: 5 minutes :: Cook time: 25 minutes

The fresh sage and garlic flavors really come through in this pork chop recipe. The potatoes go very well with the pork.

FOR THE PORK CHOPS

4 tablespoons butter, divided

1 tablespoon vegetable oil

4 (1½-inch thick) bone-in pork rib chops

Salt

Freshly ground black pepper

7 sage sprigs

2 garlic cloves, peeled and smashed

FOR THE POTATOES

½ pound baby red potatoes, halved

½ cup milk

TO MAKE THE PORK CHOPS

1. Heat 2 tablespoons of butter and oil in a large cast iron pan over medium-high heat.
2. Season the pork chops with salt and pepper.
3. Cook the pork chops for 3 to 4 minutes per side until browned. Place the sage and garlic in the pan for the last 2 minutes of cooking.
4. Check for doneness; the pork chops should read 135°F with an instant thermometer.

TO MAKE THE POTATOES

5. Place the potatoes in a pot of water and boil for 8 to 10 minutes, or until tender.
6. Drain the potatoes and stir in the milk and remaining 2 tablespoons of butter. Then mash the potatoes using a potato masher. Season with salt and pepper and serve alongside the pork chops.

Recipe tip: If you don't have sage, feel free to use rosemary or thyme instead. The flavor will be different but still delicious.

Per serving: Total calories: 477; Total fat: 30g; Carbohydrates: 29g; Fiber: 3g; Sugars: 4g; Protein: 24g

GRILLED PORK TENDERLOIN WITH FRUIT SALSA

DAIRY-FREE, NUT-FREE, SOY-FREE

Serves 6 :: Prep time: 10 minutes :: Cook time: 20 minutes

I get a lot of requests to make this dish every time we visit relatives in New York. They think it's world-class eating!

FOR THE PORK TENDERLOIN

2 tablespoons extra-virgin olive oil

4 garlic cloves, minced

1 teaspoon chili powder

1 teaspoon ground cumin

2 pork tenderloins (about 3 pounds total), trimmed

½ teaspoon salt

½ teaspoon freshly ground black pepper

FOR THE FRUIT SALSA

1 medium purple plum, halved and pitted

1 medium peach, halved and pitted

1 medium apricot, halved and pitted

1 red onion, cut into ½-inch-thick rounds

1 tablespoon extra-virgin olive oil

Salt

Freshly ground black pepper

2 tablespoons chopped fresh cilantro

1 tablespoon lime juice

1. Heat the grill to medium heat.
2. Combine the oil, garlic, chili powder, and cumin in a small bowl.
3. Season the tenderloins with salt and pepper, and then rub the seasoning evenly over the pork.
4. Place the pork on the grill and cover, turning the pork every 1½ minutes, until an instant thermometer inserted in the thickest part registers 145°F, about 15 minutes.
5. Transfer the pork to a cutting board and let it rest while you grill the fruit.
6. Brush the fruit and onion with the oil and sprinkle salt and pepper.
7. Grill the fruit and onion for 3 to 4 minutes per side, or until tender and grill-marked. Remove from the grill and coarsely chop. Transfer to a bowl and add the cilantro and lime juice. Adjust salt and pepper as needed.
8. Slice the pork diagonally and serve with the fruit salsa.

Recipe tip: Alternatively, sear the tenderloin in a large cast iron pan on all sides and roast in a 400°F oven for 20 minutes.

Per serving: Total calories: 349; Total fat: 15g; Carbohydrates: 7g; Fiber: 1g; Sugars: 4g; Protein: 49g

KIELBASA, POTATO, AND PEPPER SUPPER

NUT-FREE, SOY-FREE

Serves 6 :: Prep time: 10 minutes :: Cook time: 15 minutes

This dish is a medley of vegetable and potatoes with smoky bits of kielbasa. The potatoes are the star with nutritious onions, peppers, and zucchini added for a well-rounded supper.

- 1 pound baby red potatoes, halved
- 2 tablespoons butter
- 2 tablespoons extra-virgin olive oil
- 1 Polish kielbasa, sliced into bite-size pieces
- 1 red onion, coarsely chopped
- 2 garlic cloves, minced
- 2 bell peppers (any color), coarsely chopped
- 2 medium zucchini, coarsely chopped
- Salt
- Freshly ground black pepper

1. Place the potatoes in a microwaveable bowl and add enough water to cover. Microwave for 6 to 8 minutes, or until slightly tender, then drain the potatoes and set them aside.
2. In a large cast iron pan, add the butter and oil. Sauté the kielbasa until it starts to brown; transfer it to a plate.
3. Next, in the same pan, sauté the onion for 3 minutes. Then add the garlic and bell peppers. Stir frequently for 3 to 5 minutes, or until the peppers start to brown on the edges.
4. Add the potatoes, zucchini, and kielbasa. Cook for about 5 minutes, and then season with salt and pepper and serve.

Per serving: Total calories: 355; Total fat: 26g; Carbohydrates: 21g; Fiber: 3g; Sugars: 5g; Protein: 11g

ROSEMARY-GARLIC AND CITRUS MARINATED GRILLED LAMB CHOPS

DAIRY-FREE, NUT-FREE, SOY-FREE

Serves 4 :: Prep time: 15 minutes :: Cook time: 15 minutes

The aroma of the rosemary and garlic in this dish makes it irresistible. This recipe has all the makings of a special dinner with friends and family.

8 to 10 lamb loin chops

Salt

Freshly ground black pepper

3 tablespoons lemon juice

2 tablespoons extra-virgin olive oil

4 garlic cloves, minced

1 tablespoon lemon zest

4 rosemary sprigs

1. Season the lamb with salt and pepper.
2. Combine all the other ingredients except the rosemary in a bowl.
3. Place the lamb chops and rosemary in a large resealable plastic bag and add the lemon juice mixture. Mix well and let it marinate in the refrigerator for up to 1 day.
4. Take the chops out of the refrigerator 30 minutes before you plan to grill.
5. Grill at medium-high heat for 3 to 4 minutes per side, or until the internal temperature reaches 120°F for rare, 125°F for medium rare, 130°F for medium, and 145°F or higher for well done.

Recipe tip: You don't have to marinate this all day, but if you have the time, I think it makes the dish taste even better.

Per serving: Total calories: 224; Total fat: 14g; Carbohydrates: 2g; Fiber: 1g; Sugars: <1g; Protein: 22g

HERB-CRUSTED RACKS OF LAMB

DAIRY-FREE, NUT-FREE, SOY-FREE

Serves 4 :: Prep time: 3 minutes :: Cook time: 25 minutes

Wow your guests or family with this one. Everyone will think you spent hours in the kitchen when they taste the delicate flavors of the herb-and-onion crunchy rub on this rack of lamb.

2 racks of lamb (8 ribs each), at room temperature

FOR THE HERB SEASONING

1 medium onion, finely chopped

¼ cup gluten-free fine bread crumbs

2 teaspoons minced fresh oregano or 1 teaspoon dried oregano

1 tablespoon chopped fresh dill or 1 teaspoon dried dill

1 teaspoon salt

⅛ teaspoon freshly ground black pepper

1. Preheat the oven to 425°F.
2. Combine all the seasoning ingredients in a bowl. Pat seasoning on the lamb.
3. Place the lamb on a broiler rack in a roasting pan.
4. Roast for about 25 minutes for medium rare. Cook longer according to your preference.

Recipe tip: Ask your butcher to remove the chine bone (back bone) and excess fat.

Per serving: Total calories: 579; Total fat: 44g; Carbohydrates: 13g; Fiber: 1g; Sugars: 2g; Protein: 33g

GRILLED LOADED FLANK STEAKS WITH CORN SALSA

DAIRY-FREE, NUT-FREE

Serves 6 :: Prep time: 15 minutes :: Cook time: 15 minutes

Flank steak with a Cajun twist! The spicy char is wonderfully highlighted by the corn salsa. The salsa itself has a great sweetness that gets some bite from the jalapeño pepper and a touch of acidity from the tomatoes that complements the steak.

FOR THE FLANK STEAK

2 pounds flank steak

1½ tablespoons Homemade Cajun Seasoning (page 134)

1 teaspoon canola oil or nonstick cooking spray, for greasing

FOR THE CORN SALSA

1 (16-ounce) bag frozen corn

2 medium cucumbers, peeled, seeded, and diced

1 cup cherry tomatoes, halved

⅓ red onion, diced

⅓ cup chopped fresh cilantro

2 tablespoons extra-virgin olive oil

2 jalapeños, thinly sliced

Juice of ½ lime

Salt

Freshly ground black pepper

1. Rub the Homemade Cajun Seasoning over the flank steak on both sides.
2. On a heated grill or large grill pan greased with canola oil, grill the steak until it starts to char slightly, about 3 minutes per side. Transfer to a cutting board and let it rest while you prepare the salsa.
3. Prepare the corn according to the package directions.
4. Combine the corn, cucumbers, tomatoes, onion, cilantro, oil, jalapeños, lime juice, and season with salt and pepper.
5. Cut the steak against the grain and top with the corn salsa before serving.

Recipe tip: This can also be prepared with the All-Purpose Dry Rub (page 133).

Per serving: Total calories: 354; Total fat: 16g; Carbohydrates: 18g; Fiber: 3g; Sugars: 5g; Protein: 35g

GRILLED STEAKS WITH MUSHROOM SAUCE

Serves 4 :: Prep time: 15 minutes :: Cook time: 15 minutes

This steak entrée and its creamy, savory sauce will be a hit. The garlic gives the cream sauce body and flavor, while the Worcestershire sauce gives the sauce its savory taste.

4 New York strip steaks, about 1-inch thick

Salt

Freshly ground black pepper

2 tablespoons extra-virgin olive oil

2 tablespoons butter

4 garlic cloves, smashed, divided

1 rosemary sprig

8 ounces sliced white button mushrooms

½ cup heavy cream

2 teaspoons gluten-free Worcestershire sauce

1. Season the steaks with salt and pepper.
2. Heat a large cast iron pan over medium-high heat and add the oil and butter. Add the steaks to the pan in batches and cook the steaks for about 3 minutes per side, or until browned.
3. Reduce the heat to medium-low and add 2 garlic cloves and the rosemary. Baste the steaks with the liquid from the pan while continuing to cook for another 1 to 2 minutes.
4. Remove the garlic and rosemary and transfer the steak to a plate.

5. Mince the remaining 2 garlic cloves and sauté until fragrant, then add the mushrooms. Cook the mushrooms for about 4 minutes, or until soft, and then add the cream and Worcestershire sauce. Let simmer while stirring and season with salt and pepper.
6. Spoon the mushroom sauce over the steaks and serve.

Per serving: Total calories: 456; Total fat: 38g; Carbohydrates: 4g; Fiber: 1g; Sugars: 3g; Protein: 28g

How to Cook a Steak

Here are some tips for achieving different levels of steak doneness for 1-inch steaks.

Rare: Grill for 5 minutes, turn, and grill for another 3 minutes, or until internal temperature reads 120 to 130°F.

Medium rare: Grill for 5 minutes, turn, and grill for another 4 minutes, or until internal temperature reads 130 to 135°F.

Medium: Grill for 6 minutes, turn, and grill for another 5 minutes, or until internal temperature reads 140 to 150°F.

Medium well: Grill for 7 minutes, turn, and grill for another 5 minutes, or until internal temperature reads 155 to 165°F.

Well done: Grill for 10 to 12 minutes per side, or until temperature reads 170°F.

PRESSURE COOKER BEEF STEW

DAIRY-FREE, NUT-FREE, SOY-FREE

Serves 6 :: Prep time: 10 minutes :: Cook time: 20 minutes

Beef stew in 30 minutes? Yes, it can be done! This hearty and meaty beef stew is a great dinner for chilly nights. Traditional yet tasty, this stew is even better as leftovers.

2 pounds beef stew meat

Salt

Freshly ground black pepper

2 tablespoons cornstarch

2 to 3 tablespoons water

1 (1.3-ounce) package gluten-free beef stew seasoning

2 tablespoons extra-virgin olive oil

4 large carrots, peeled and diced

2 large potatoes, peeled and diced

8 ounces green beans, trimmed

8 ounces sliced white mushrooms

Salt

Freshly ground black pepper

1. Season the beef with salt and pepper.
2. Whisk the cornstarch in the water and set aside.
3. Heat a pressure cooker over medium-high heat. Add the oil and stew meat and brown for about 3 minutes. Add enough water to cover the meat, add the beef stew seasoning, and stir. Put on the lid of the pressure cooker and cook for 15 minutes. Follow the manufacturer's instructions for your specific cooker.
4. Reduce the pressure, add the vegetables and mushrooms, and season with salt and pepper. Stir to mix; if you need more water, this is the time to add it.
5. Cover the cooker again and cook for 3 minutes. Stir in the cornstarch slurry and adjust the seasoning accordingly.

Per serving: Total calories: 403; Total fat: 13g; Carbohydrates: 34g; Fiber: 5g; Sugars: 5g; Protein: 38g

EASY SLOPPY JOES

Serves 6 :: Prep time: 10 minutes :: Cook time: 20 minutes

This classic recipe is one of the easiest to prepare while also being so delicious and satisfying. It's kid-friendly, too.

1 tablespoon extra-virgin olive oil

1 large onion, diced

3 garlic cloves, minced

2 pounds lean ground beef

¼ cup brown sugar

1 tablespoon steak seasoning

1 large bell pepper, chopped

3 tablespoons gluten-free Worcestershire sauce

1 tablespoon red wine vinegar

2 (15-ounce) cans tomato sauce

3 tablespoons tomato paste

Salt

Freshly ground black pepper

½ cup shredded Cheddar cheese

Gluten-free hamburger buns, for serving

1. Heat a large skillet over medium heat. Add the oil, onion, and garlic, and sauté for 3 to 5 minutes, or until the onions are soft.
2. Add the beef and cook until browned, then add the sugar and steak seasoning.
3. Stir in the bell peppers, Worcestershire sauce, and vinegar. Stir and simmer for 5 minutes, then add the tomato sauce and paste. Season with salt and pepper, and simmer the mixture for another 5 minutes until slightly thickened.
4. Serve on the buns and top with the Cheddar cheese.

Recipe tip: To make this dairy-free, you can omit the cheese.

Per serving (without buns): Total calories: 428; Total fat: 21g; Carbohydrates: 27g; Fiber: 4g; Sugars: 15g; Protein: 36g

BARBECUE MEAT LOAF

NUT-FREE

Serves 2 :: Prep time: 5 minutes :: Cook time: 25 minutes

Combining this traditional, family-pleasing meat loaf with barbecue sauce and onions makes a great dinner. Even the pickiest of eaters will enjoy this barbecue-inspired take on the classic.

- ¼ cup chopped onion
- 2 teaspoons vegetable oil, divided
- 1 pound ground chuck
- ½ cup barbecue sauce, divided
- ½ cup shredded Parmesan cheese
- ¼ cup gluten-free Italian bread crumbs
- 1 egg
- 2 tablespoons chopped fresh parsley
- ¼ teaspoon salt
- ¼ teaspoon freshly ground black pepper

1. Preheat the oven to 375°F.
2. Sauté the onion in 1 teaspoon of oil until soft, or about 3 minutes.
3. In a large bowl, combine all the ingredients, except ¼ cup of barbecue sauce and the remaining oil, until well blended.
4. Grease a baking pan with the remaining 1 teaspoon of oil. Shape the mixture into a loaf and place on the prepared pan. Spread the remaining barbecue sauce on top of the loaf and bake for about 25 minutes, or until fully cooked.

Per serving: Total calories: 797; Total fat: 56g; Carbohydrates: 19g; Fiber: 2g; Sugars: 22g; Protein: 55g

HAMBURGER WITH MUSHROOM AND FUSILLI PASTA

NUT-FREE

Serves 4 :: Prep time: 10 minutes :: Cook time: 20 minutes

A creamy and delicious pasta dish. This tastes just as good for leftovers—if there are any. The curly fusilli isn't necessary, but I think it adds a fun touch.

1 pound lean ground beef

1 tablespoon extra-virgin olive oil

1 pound cremini mushrooms, thinly sliced

Salt

Freshly ground black pepper

2 tablespoons tomato paste

1 tablespoon gluten-free all-purpose flour

1 (32-ounce) box beef broth

1 (12-ounce) package gluten-free fusilli pasta

½ cup sour cream

1 teaspoon Dijon mustard

2 tablespoons fresh parsley, chopped

1. Brown the beef in a large pan for about 3 minutes. Drain the excess liquid and transfer to a bowl.
2. In the same pan, add the oil and the mushrooms; sauté for 5 minutes, stirring occasionally, and season with salt and pepper.
3. Return the beef to the pan. Then stir in the tomato paste and flour and cook for 1 minute.
4. Add the broth and pasta to the pan. Bring to a boil, and then lower the heat. Cover and simmer for about 10 minutes, stirring occasionally.
5. Add the sour cream and mustard and stir to blend. Garnish with the parsley and season with salt and pepper as needed.

Recipe tip: Gluten-free penne and elbow pasta are good substitutes if you can't find gluten-free fusilli.

Per serving: Total calories: 663; Total fat: 21g; Carbohydrates: 81g; Fiber: 7g; Sugars: 7g; Protein: 41g

TERIYAKI BEEF WITH RICE NOODLES

DAIRY-FREE, NUT-FREE

Serves 4 :: Prep time: 5 minutes :: Cook time: 15 minutes

This dish is great for satisfying that craving for Asian food. It makes for a tasty lunch or dinner for the whole family. The sweet-and-salty mix of the teriyaki is sure to please.

6 ounces rice noodles

1 pound lean boneless beef sirloin or eye of round steak

Salt

Freshly ground black pepper

¼ cup tamari or gluten-free soy sauce

2 tablespoons brown sugar

1 tablespoon cornstarch

1 teaspoon sesame oil

2 tablespoons vegetable oil

2 garlic cloves, minced

1 teaspoon fresh ginger, grated

¼ cup water (optional)

1. Cook the rice noodles according to the package directions and set aside.
2. Thinly cut the steak against the grain. Season with salt and pepper.
3. In a small bowl, combine tamari, brown sugar, cornstarch, and sesame oil. Set aside.
4. Heat a large skillet over medium-high heat and add the vegetable oil.
5. Sauté the garlic and ginger for 20 seconds until fragrant, then add the beef. Cook beef for 2 to 3 minutes. Then stir in the noodles, pour in the tamari mixture, and stir to blend. If the mixture is too dry, add the water. Cook for another 2 minutes and adjust the seasoning with salt and pepper.

Per serving: Total calories: 385; Total fat: 13g; Carbohydrates: 39g; Fiber: 1g; Sugars: 5g; Protein: 31g

SZECHUAN BEEF WITH SNOW PEAS

DAIRY-FREE, NUT-FREE

Serves 4 :: Prep time: 10 minutes :: Cook time: 15 minutes

This is a popular Chinese dish. Serve with jasmine rice and top with sliced scallions and toasted sesame seeds.

- 1 pound boneless beef steak (sirloin, top loin, or rib eye)
- 6 tablespoons tamari or gluten-free soy sauce, divided
- 1 tablespoon cornstarch, divided
- 2 tablespoons cooking sherry
- 2 garlic cloves, minced
- ½ cup water
- ½ teaspoon crushed red pepper flakes
- 2 tablespoons vegetable oil, divided
- 1 onion, sliced into wedges
- 8 ounces fresh snow peas, trimmed
- Salt
- Freshly ground black pepper
- 2 medium tomatoes, cut into wedges
- 2 sliced scallions, for garnish
- 1 teaspoon toasted sesame seeds, for garnish

1. Slice the steak across the grain into thin strips.
2. In a medium bowl, combine 3 tablespoons of tamari, ½ tablespoon of cornstarch, the sherry, and garlic; stir in the beef and let it stand for a few minutes.
3. Meanwhile, combine the water, the remaining ½ tablespoon of cornstarch, the remaining 3 tablespoons of tamari, and the red pepper flakes.
4. Heat 1 tablespoon of oil in a wok over high heat. Add the beef and cook for about 1 minute, then transfer to a plate.
5. In the same wok, add the remaining 1 tablespoon of oil and sauté the onions for 2 minutes. Stir in the snow peas and season with salt and pepper.
6. Return beef to the pan and add the mixture of water, cornstarch, tamari, and red pepper flakes, as well as the tomatoes. Stir and cook for about 2 minutes, or until the sauce thickens and the tomatoes are heated through. Top with the scallions and sesame seeds.

Recipe tip: You can easily double this recipe and save the extras for an especially busy weeknight. It's even tastier as leftovers!

Per serving: Total calories: 268; Total fat: 12g; Carbohydrates: 16g; Fiber: 2g; Sugars: 4g; Protein: 31g

CHAPTER NINE

DESSERTS AND SWEET TREATS

Chocolate Mousse with Fresh Whipped Cream 120

Gooey Turtle Bars 121

Double Chocolate Chip Cookies 122

Churros with Chocolate Dipping Sauce 123

Marvelous Coconut Macaroons 124

Tapioca Pudding 125

Candied Apple Skewers 126

Lemon Curd with Mixed Berries 127

Fresh Peach Cobbler 128

Baked Apricots with Honey and Almonds 129

< Churros with Chocolate Dipping Sauce, page 123

CHOCOLATE MOUSSE WITH FRESH WHIPPED CREAM

VEGETARIAN, NUT-FREE

Serves 8 :: Prep time: 5 minutes :: Cook time: 10 minutes

This quick chocolate mousse is so smooth, and it's one of the easiest desserts to make. Pick a good-quality chocolate—it makes a lot of difference in taste.

FOR THE MOUSSE

5¼ ounces good-quality semisweet chocolate, chopped

14 ounces cold heavy whipping cream

3 large egg whites

2 tablespoons sugar

Sweetened whipped cream, for serving (see following recipe)

Shaved bittersweet or semisweet chocolate, for garnish

FOR THE WHIPPED TOPPING

1 cup heavy whipping cream

1 tablespoon sugar

1 teaspoon vanilla extract

TO MAKE THE MOUSSE

1. Place the chocolate in a double boiler over low heat and stir until melted. Remove from heat and let stand.
2. Beat the heavy whipping cream with a handheld mixer until soft peaks form. Set aside.
3. In a bowl, beat the egg whites until soft peaks form. Gradually add the sugar and continue whipping until firm.
4. Fold the egg whites into the still-warm chocolate until fully incorporated.
5. Fold the chocolate mixture into the whipped cream. Cover the mousse with plastic wrap and refrigerate until ready to serve.

TO MAKE THE WHIPPED TOPPING

Pour the whipping cream into a bowl and beat with a handheld mixer until it starts to thicken, then add the sugar and vanilla. Continue whipping until firm, about 3 minutes. Serve on top of the mousse.

Recipe tip: You can also use bittersweet chocolate in place of semisweet. Just remember: the higher the cacao percentage, the less sweet the chocolate.

Per serving: Total calories: 398; Total fat: 36g; Carbohydrates: 19g; Fiber: 1g; Sugars: 17g; Protein: 4g

GOOEY TURTLE BARS

VEGETARIAN

Serves 6 :: Prep time: 10 minutes :: Cook time: 15 minutes

Get ready for a new family favorite. These sweet turtle bars are great for munching and snacking!

2 cups gluten-free graham crackers

½ cup butter, melted

2 cups semisweet chocolate morsels

1 cup pecans, chopped

1 (12-ounce) jar caramel topping

1. Preheat the oven to 350°F.
2. Pulse the graham crackers in a food processor until crumbled.
3. Combine the graham cracker crumbs and butter in a bowl. Press firmly into the bottom of a 9-by-13-inch baking pan. Sprinkle with the chocolate morsels and pecans.
4. Microwave the caramel and drizzle over the baking pan.
5. Bake for about 15 minutes, or until the chocolate morsels have melted; let cool in the pan.
6. Once the bars have reached a workable temperature, cut into bars.

Recipe tip: You can use peanuts instead of pecans if you prefer.

Per serving: Total calories: 873; Total fat: 51g; Carbohydrates: 111g; Fiber: 7g; Sugars: 66g; Protein: 9g

DOUBLE CHOCOLATE CHIP COOKIES

VEGETARIAN

Makes 12 cookies :: Prep time: 20 minutes :: Cook time: 9 minutes

These classic cookies are so good, they disappear practically overnight from my cookie jar. Everyone loves them!

- 1 cup gluten-free all-purpose flour
- ¾ cup unsweetened cocoa powder
- ½ teaspoon baking soda
- ½ teaspoon gluten-free baking powder
- 1 teaspoon salt
- ¾ cup brown sugar
- ⅔ cup granulated sugar
- 10 tablespoons butter, at room temperature
- 1 egg
- 2 teaspoons vanilla extract
- 2 cups semisweet chocolate morsels

1. In a medium bowl, mix the flour, cocoa powder, baking soda, baking powder, and salt.
2. In another bowl, combine the brown sugar, granulated sugar, and butter. Beat with a handheld mixer until very light, about 3 minutes. Add the egg and vanilla and beat until well combined.
3. Combine the dry ingredients and the butter-and-sugar mixture. Mix on low until just combined, and then fold in the chocolate morsels. Cover and refrigerate.
4. Preheat the oven to 375°F.
5. Line a large baking sheet with parchment paper. Form the dough into 12 equal balls.
6. Bake for about 8 to 9 minutes. Let the cookies cool before serving.

Recipe tip: If you are using self-rising flour, omit the baking powder and salt.

Per serving (1 cookie): Total calories: 353; Total fat: 20g; Carbohydrates: 52g; Fiber: 5g; Sugars: 36g; Protein: 4g

CHURROS WITH CHOCOLATE DIPPING SAUCE

VEGETARIAN

Serves 4 :: Prep time: 10 minutes :: Cook time: 20 minutes

Homemade churros are simply the best, hands down. They're crispy on the outside and soft in the inside. The chocolate dipping sauce makes this sweet treat irresistible.

FOR THE CHURROS

½ cup sugar

1 teaspoon ground cinnamon

Cooking oil, for frying

1 cup water

1 stick butter (8 tablespoons)

¼ teaspoon salt

1 cup gluten-free all-purpose flour

3 large eggs, beaten

FOR THE CHOCOLATE DIPPING SAUCE

½ cup heavy cream

3½ ounces dark chocolate, chopped

1. In a shallow bowl, mix the sugar and cinnamon and set aside.
2. Heat about 3 inches of oil in a deep fryer or heavy-bottom pan to 360°F.
3. Meanwhile, in another saucepan, combine the water, butter, and salt. Bring to a boil over high heat. Add the flour and reduce the heat to low, stirring vigorously, about 1 minute.
4. Turn off the heat and stir in the eggs, stirring constantly for 2 to 3 minutes.
5. Spoon the dough into a pastry bag. Cut the tip and squeeze about 5 inches in length into the hot oil, using scissors to cut the dough. You can cook 5 to 7 churros at a time depending on the size of your deep fryer or pan. Fry for 3 to 4 minutes, or until golden brown. Transfer them to a plate with paper towels to drain excess oil.
6. Roll the cooked churros in the sugar and cinnamon mixture.
7. For the dipping sauce, warm the heavy cream in a saucepan (making sure not to boil), then remove from heat and add the chocolate. Let it sit for 1 minute, and then stir to combine.

Recipe tip: Always be careful when deep-frying; hot oil can easily spatter.

Per serving: Total calories: 767; Total fat: 46g; Carbohydrates: 89g; Fiber: 5g; Sugars: 64g; Protein: 10g

MARVELOUS COCONUT MACAROONS

VEGETARIAN, SOY-FREE

Makes 12 macaroons :: Prep time: 8 minutes :: Cook time: 20 minutes

You only need five ingredients to make these marvelous macaroons. Crisp and golden brown on the outside and soft and chewy on the inside, they're delicious all over.

1 (14-ounce) bag sweetened angel flaked coconut

¾ cup plus 2 tablespoons sweetened condensed milk

1 teaspoon vanilla extract

¼ teaspoon salt

2 egg whites

1. Preheat the oven to 325°F.
2. Line a large baking sheet with parchment paper.
3. In a medium bowl, combine the coconut, condensed milk, vanilla, and salt.
4. In another bowl, beat the egg whites using a handheld mixer on high until soft peaks form.
5. Mix the egg whites and the coconut mixture together.
6. Scoop 2 spoonfuls of the mixture and form mounds on the prepared pan, allowing about 1 inch of space from one another.
7. Bake for 20 minutes, or until golden brown. Remove from the oven and let the macaroons cool on a wire rack.

Per serving (1 macaroon): Total calories: 231; Total fat: 13g; Carbohydrates: 27g; Fiber: 2g; Sugars: 24g; Protein: 2g

TAPIOCA PUDDING

VEGAN, DAIRY-FREE, NUT-FREE, SOY-FREE

Serves 4 :: Prep time: 5 minutes :: Cook time: 15 minutes

This tapioca pudding uses small pearl tapioca with coconut cream and Asian fruits. I consider this comfort food—it was one of my favorites growing up.

½ cup small tapioca pearls

2 cups water

½ cup coconut cream

½ cup sugar

¼ teaspoon salt

1 cup assorted canned Thai fruits, sliced (coconut meat, jackfruit, lychee)

1. Place the tapioca in a medium saucepan and rinse well. Add the water and bring to a boil, stirring constantly. Reduce to a simmer and cook for 15 minutes, or until all the pearls are soft and clear.
2. Stir in the coconut cream, sugar, and salt.
3. Add the sliced fruits and some of the syrup if needed for a thinner consistency, and serve.

Recipe tip: If you can't find canned Thai fruits, you can substitute with sliced mangos and berries.

Per serving: Total calories: 246; Total fat: 6g; Carbohydrates: 46g; Fiber: 1g; Sugars: 28g; Protein: 3g

CANDIED APPLE SKEWERS

VEGETARIAN

Serves 6 :: Prep time: 20 minutes :: Cook time: 5 minutes

These apples on skewers are fun to make and very delicious. They are an especially great idea for Halloween, since they're lighter and more manageable than whole caramel apples.

3 Granny Smith apples, cored and quartered

Juice of 1 lemon

½ pound caramel

2 tablespoons cream

½ cup peanuts, finely chopped

1. Skewer 1 slice of apple lollipop style to make 12 apple "lollipops."
2. Squeeze the lemon juice over the apples to prevent browning. Line a platter with parchment paper.
3. Combine the caramel and cream in a microwave-safe bowl. Microwave in 30-second increments, stirring between each session, until the caramel has melted. Stir until smooth.
4. Dip the apples into the caramel, letting the excess drip off. Arrange the apples on the prepared platter. Repeat until all apples are coated with caramel.
5. Sprinkle the peanuts over the apples.

Recipe tip: You can omit the peanuts or replace them with something else, such as chocolate chips or toasted coconut, if you have a nut allergy.

Per serving: Total calories: 271; Total fat: 11g; Carbohydrates: 42g; Fiber: 3g; Sugars: 33g; Protein: 5g

LEMON CURD WITH MIXED BERRIES

VEGETARIAN, SOY-FREE

Serves 6 :: Prep time: 15 minutes :: Cook time: 10 minutes

This tart lemon dessert is so tasty, especially with fresh berries. I use a mix, but you can use whatever berries you have on hand.

- 6 large egg yolks, lightly beaten
- ¾ cup fresh lemon juice (about 6 or 7 lemons)
- ½ cup sugar
- ⅛ teaspoon salt
- 1½ tablespoons butter, cut into small pieces
- 2 teaspoons lemon zest
- 1 cup sliced fresh strawberries
- 1 cup fresh blueberries
- 1 cup fresh raspberries

1. In a small heavy saucepan, combine the egg yolks, lemon juice, sugar, and salt. Cook over medium heat until a candy thermometer reads 160°F or until thick, about 6 minutes, stirring constantly with a whisk.
2. Remove from heat and then add the butter and lemon zest, stirring until the butter melts.
3. Combine the berries in a bowl.
4. Divide the lemon curd among dessert bowls. Top with the berries and serve.

Recipe tip: Save the egg whites for another recipe like Marvelous Coconut Macaroons (page 124). Egg whites will usually stay good for 2 to 4 days in the refrigerator and up to 1 year in the freezer.

Per serving: Total calories: 184; Total fat: 8g; Carbohydrates: 28g; Fiber: 3g; Sugars: 22g; Protein: 3g

FRESH PEACH COBBLER

VEGETARIAN

Serves 4 :: Prep time: 5 minutes :: Cook time: 25 minutes

Whenever I have a craving for a tasty, old-fashioned dessert, this fresh cobbler is always on the top of my list. I love serving it for guests as well.

- 4 cups fresh peaches (about 6 medium peaches), pitted, peeled, and sliced
- ½ cup granulated sugar, plus 1 tablespoon
- 1 tablespoon cornstarch
- ¼ teaspoon ground nutmeg
- 1 teaspoon lemon juice
- 1 cup gluten-free all-purpose flour
- 3 tablespoons shortening
- 1½ teaspoon gluten-free baking powder
- ½ teaspoon salt
- ½ cup milk
- ¼ teaspoon ground cinnamon

1. Preheat the oven to 400°F.
2. Boil water in a pot, add ½ cup of peaches for 30 seconds, remove, then dip them in cold water. Peel and slice the peaches.
3. In a 2-quart saucepan, mix ½ cup of sugar, cornstarch, and nutmeg. Stir in the peaches and lemon juice. Cook over medium heat for 2 to 3 minutes, stirring constantly, or until the mixture boils and thickens. Cook for 1 minute and then pour to into an ungreased 2-quart casserole dish.
4. Cut the shortening into the flour, the remaining 1 tablespoon of sugar, baking powder, and salt until the mixture resembles fine crumbs. Stir in the milk, and then drop the dough by spoonfuls into the hot peach mixture. Sprinkle the cinnamon over the dough.
5. Bake for about 25 minutes, or until the topping is golden brown. Serve warm with vanilla ice cream if desired.

Recipe tip: You can substitute 2 packages (16 ounces each) of frozen sliced peaches, thawed and drained well, if peaches aren't in season near you.

Per serving: Total calories: 381; Total fat: 11g; Carbohydrates: 70g; Fiber: 6g; Sugars: 43g; Protein: 5g

BAKED APRICOTS WITH HONEY AND ALMONDS

VEGETARIAN, SOY-FREE

Serves 4 :: Prep time: 5 minutes :: Cook time: 15 minutes

These baked apricots smell so good while baking, and they taste even better. The juicy apricot and the crunchiness of the almond contrast each other so nicely. They never last long at my house.

Butter, for greasing

4 ripe apricots, halved and pitted

¼ cup honey

¼ cup slivered almonds

¼ teaspoon ground ginger

¼ teaspoon ground nutmeg

1. Preheat the oven to 400°F and grease a large baking pan with butter.
2. Arrange the apricots in a single layer on the prepared pan, cut-sides up. Drizzle the honey over the apricots, and sprinkle with the almonds, ginger, and nutmeg.
3. Bake for 12 to 15 minutes, or until the apricots are tender and the almonds are golden brown.

Recipe tip: These apricots go well with a scoop (or two) of ice cream on the side.

Per serving: Total calories: 121; Total fat: 4g; Carbohydrates: 23g; Fiber: 2g; Sugars: 21g; Protein: 2g

CHAPTER TEN

SEASONINGS, SAUCES, AND STAPLES

Italian Seasoning 132

All-Purpose Dry Rub 133

Homemade Cajun Seasoning 134

Thick Teriyaki Sauce 135

Fresh Roasted Tomato Sauce 136

Tartar Sauce 137

Sweet-and-Sour Sauce 138

Barbecue Sauce 139

Basic No-Knead Pizza Crust 140

Gluten-Free Baking Mix 141

< Italian Seasoning, page 132
All-Purpose Dry Rub, page 133
Homemade Cajun Seasoning, page 134

ITALIAN SEASONING

Makes 10 tablespoons :: Prep time: 3 minutes

VEGAN, DAIRY-FREE, NUT-FREE, SOY-FREE

Consisting of dried herbs and spices, this Italian seasoning is perfect for pasta dishes. It's also great for chicken, pork, beef, vegetables, salads, and soups. This blend is so simple, you will never go back to the store-bought variety again.

3 tablespoons dried parsley

3 tablespoons dried basil

2 tablespoons dried oregano

1 tablespoon garlic powder

1 teaspoon dried rosemary

1 teaspoon dried thyme

1 teaspoon onion powder

½ teaspoon freshly ground black pepper

½ teaspoon red pepper flakes

1. Combine all the ingredients in a food processor. Process until desired consistency is achieved.
2. Store in an airtight container for up to 1 year.

Per serving (1 tablespoon): Total calories: 12; Total fat: <1g; Carbohydrates: 3g; Fiber: 1g; Sugars: <1g; Protein: 1g

ALL-PURPOSE DRY RUB

VEGAN, DAIRY-FREE, NUT-FREE, SOY-FREE

Makes 2¾ cups :: Prep time: 5 minutes

This rub is great to use when grilling baby back ribs, chicken, and fish. The balance of spices and sugar makes it very versatile in everyday cooking as well.

- ⅓ cup smoked paprika
- ¼ cup freshly ground black pepper
- ¼ cup brown sugar
- ¼ cup chili powder
- ¼ cup kosher salt
- 3 tablespoons ground cumin
- 2 tablespoons ground coriander
- 1 tablespoon cayenne pepper

Combine all the ingredients in a bowl and mix well. Store in an airtight spice container for up to 1 year.

Per serving (¼ cup): Total calories: 44; Total fat: 1g; Carbohydrates: 11g; Fiber: 4g; Sugars: 4g; Protein: 2g

HOMEMADE CAJUN SEASONING

VEGAN, DAIRY-FREE, NUT-FREE, SOY-FREE

Makes 12 tablespoons :: Prep time: 5 minutes

This Cajun seasoning is great on chicken, meat, and fish. Add some Louisiana flavor to your dishes.

- 3 tablespoons paprika
- 2 tablespoons garlic powder
- 2 tablespoons fine kosher salt
- 1 tablespoon freshly ground black pepper
- 1 tablespoon ground white pepper
- 1 tablespoon dried oregano
- 1 tablespoon onion powder
- 1 tablespoon cayenne pepper
- 2 teaspoons dried thyme

Mix all the ingredients in a bowl. Store in an airtight container for up to 1 year.

Per serving (1 tablespoon): Total calories: 17; Total fat: <1g; Carbohydrates: 4g; Fiber: 2g; Sugars: <1g; Protein: <1g

THICK TERIYAKI SAUCE

VEGAN, DAIRY-FREE, NUT-FREE

Makes 1½ cups :: Prep time: 5 minutes :: Cook time: 15 minutes

Sticky and spicy, this sauce is a great marinade as well as a glaze. Fresh homemade sauce with all-natural ingredients beats the bottled stuff any day of the week.

2 tablespoons vegetable oil

1 teaspoon sesame oil

2 garlic cloves, minced

1 inch fresh ginger, grated

⅓ cup brown sugar

⅔ cup tamari or gluten-free soy sauce

⅔ cup mirin

¼ cup sake

2 tablespoons toasted sesame seeds

1. Heat a medium saucepan over medium heat. Add the vegetable oil, sesame oil, garlic, and ginger. Sauté for about 1 minute, or until fragrant.
2. Add the brown sugar and stir for 2 minutes.
3. Stir in the tamari, mirin, and sake. Bring to a slow boil, stirring constantly until the sauce thickens, about 10 minutes. Remove from heat and add the sesame seeds.

Recipe tip: Mirin is important in this sauce. Its sweetness tempers the saltiness from the tamari or gluten-free soy sauce. You can find it in the international foods aisle of your grocery store.

Per serving (½ cup): Total calories: 346; Total fat: 14g; Carbohydrates: 53g; Fiber: 1g; Sugars: 31g; Protein: 8g

FRESH ROASTED TOMATO SAUCE

DAIRY-FREE, NUT-FREE, SOY-FREE

Makes 2½ cups :: Prep time: 10 minutes :: Cook time: 15 minutes

If you grow tomatoes in the summer, this is a good way to put them to use. Fresh and delicious, this sauce is great for pasta.

- 5 pounds tomatoes
- 4 tablespoons extra-virgin olive oil, divided
- 2 garlic cloves, halved
- 1 basil sprig or ½ teaspoon dried basil
- 1 tablespoon tomato paste
- 1 bay leaf
- ¾ teaspoon salt

1. Preheat the oven to 375°F.
2. Place the tomatoes on a roasting pan and drizzle with 2 tablespoons of oil. Roast for about 10 minutes, or until the tomatoes are blistered and slightly charred. Remove from the oven and let them sit until they are cool enough to handle. Peel the skin off the tomatoes and remove the seeds.
3. Put the tomatoes in a saucepan over high heat. Add the 2 remaining tablespoons of oil, garlic, basil, tomato paste, bay leaf, and salt. Bring to a boil, and then lower heat to a simmer.
4. Cook for 10 to 15 minutes, stirring occasionally, until the sauce is reduced to almost half. Taste and adjust the seasoning if needed.
5. Keep in the refrigerator until ready to use. It will be good for 3 to 4 days.

Recipe tip: You can make sauce with any kind of tomato, but the best ones for sauce are paste tomatoes. They usually have fewer seeds, less water, and a firm, meaty texture.

Per serving (½ cup): Total calories: 91; Total fat: 6g; Carbohydrates: 10g; Fiber: 2g; Sugars: 5g; Protein: 2g

TARTAR SAUCE

VEGETARIAN, NUT-FREE

Makes 1 cup :: Prep time: 5 minutes

When you want to impress family and friends, make this fresh tartar sauce for your fried fish dishes. When you tell them you made the tartar sauce fresh, they'll think you are a master cook!

- 1 cup mayonnaise
- 4 sweet pickles, finely chopped
- 1 tablespoon chopped fresh parsley
- 1 teaspoon lemon juice
- ¼ teaspoon freshly ground black pepper

Place all the ingredients in a food processor and process on low until well mixed. Serve with seafood.

Per serving (¼ cup): Total calories: 368; Total fat: 40g; Carbohydrates: 2g; Fiber: <1g; Sugars: 7g; Protein: 1g

SWEET-AND-SOUR SAUCE

VEGAN, DAIRY-FREE, NUT-FREE

Makes 1 cup :: Prep time: 3 minutes :: Cook time: 5 minutes

Ever get sweet-and-sour takeout and think, I could do this better? Here's your chance! Cook a wonderful sweet-and-sour dish with tofu, shrimp, chicken, or pork using this super easy to make sauce.

- ½ cup apple cider vinegar
- ½ cup packed light brown sugar
- ¼ cup water
- ¼ cup ketchup
- 1 tablespoon tamari or gluten-free soy sauce
- 1 tablespoon cornstarch

In a small saucepan, mix all the ingredients and heat on medium-low heat until the sauce thickens. Store in a jar in the refrigerator until ready to use. It will be good for 2 weeks.

Per serving (¼ cup): Total calories: 134; Total fat: 0g; Carbohydrates: 44g; Fiber: 0g; Sugars: 27g; Protein: 1g

BARBECUE SAUCE

DAIRY-FREE

Makes 1½ cups :: Prep time: 5 minutes :: Cook time: 15 minutes

This sweet and spicy barbecue sauce is perfect for backyard grilling. It goes great with baby back ribs and chicken.

- 1½ cups ketchup
- ¼ cup brown sugar
- 3 tablespoons apple cider vinegar
- 3 tablespoons molasses
- 2 tablespoons gluten-free Worcestershire sauce
- 2 teaspoons mustard
- 1 teaspoon paprika
- 1 teaspoon garlic powder
- 1 teaspoon salt
- ¼ teaspoon cayenne pepper

In a medium saucepan, mix all the ingredients together and bring to a slow boil. Lower the heat and simmer for about 15 minutes. Use immediately or store in a jar in the refrigerator for up to 1 week.

Per serving (½ cup): Total calories: 279; Total fat: <1g; Carbohydrates: 74g; Fiber: <1g; Sugars: 29g; Protein: 1g

BASIC NO-KNEAD PIZZA CRUST

VEGETARIAN, DAIRY-FREE, NUT-FREE

Makes 2 (12-inch) pizza crusts :: Prep time: 10 minutes :: Cook time: 10 minutes

This basic pizza dough recipe is easy and quick to make.

- 2 tablespoons extra-virgin olive oil, plus more for greasing
- 1 cup warm water (110 to 120°F)
- 1 tablespoon granulated sugar
- 1 packet instant dry yeast
- 3 cups gluten-free all-purpose flour, plus more for sprinkling
- 1½ teaspoon salt
- 1 teaspoon xanthan gum (omit if the flour you're using already has it)
- 1 large egg
- 1 teaspoon cider vinegar

1. Preheat the oven to 450°F and grease your pizza pan with 1 tablespoon of oil.
2. In a small bowl, combine the warm water, sugar, and yeast. Let it sit for 5 minutes until foamy.
3. In a stand mixer, mix the flour, salt, and xanthan gum. Add the egg, vinegar, 2 tablespoons of oil, and the yeast mixture. Mix on low until well blended, about 1 minute.
4. Grease a rubber spatula with oil and transfer the dough onto parchment paper.
5. Cut the dough into 2 equal parts. Carefully spread the dough on the prepared pan into a 12-inch round.
6. Bake for 8 to 10 minutes, or until the edges start to brown.
7. When you're ready to cook your favorite pizza, simply add your toppings and bake for an additional 8 to 10 minutes, or until cooked through.

Recipe tip: If you're not using the dough right away, place in a resealable bag and freeze. When ready to use, place the sealed bag in a bowl filled with warm water until thawed.

Per serving (1 crust): Total calories: 845; Total fat: 29g; Carbohydrates: 140g; Fiber: 19g; Sugars: 12g; Protein: 21g

GLUTEN-FREE BAKING MIX

VEGAN

Makes 3½ cups :: Prep time: 5 minutes

If you want to make sure your baking mix is free of gluten and want a fresh mix as a base for all kinds of baking needs, this is a great choice. This blend is good for cakes, cookies, muffins, and waffles.

1½ cups gluten-free brown rice flour

½ cup gluten-free potato starch

¼ cup tapioca flour

¼ cup gluten-free white rice flour

1 teaspoon xanthan gum (optional)

Mix all the ingredients in a bowl and keep in an airtight container until ready to use. You can keep the mix in the refrigerator for up to 6 months or in the freezer for 1 year.

Per serving (¼ cup): Total calories: 103; Total fat: 1g; Carbohydrates: 23g; Fiber: 1g; Sugars: <1g; Protein: 1g

SAMPLE MENUS

AMERICANA COOKOUT

Watermelon-Tomato Salad 24

Sweet-and-Spicy Barbecue Chicken 87

Roasted Corn on the Cob with Parmesan Cheese 50

Fresh Peach Cobbler 128

A TASTE OF MEXICO

Easy Taco Soup 32

Bean Dip 38

Sheet-Pan Chicken Fajitas 91

Churros with Chocolate Dipping Sauce 123

ASIAN INSPIRED

Grilled Chicken with Pineapple-Ginger Glaze 94

Thai Stir-Fried Noodles with Roasted Peanuts 59

Sweet-and-Sour Zucchini 46

Tapioca Pudding 125

MEATLESS MONDAY

Soba Noodles with Mushrooms, Broccoli, and Tofu 58

Veggie and Pineapple Fried Rice 60

Vegetable Fritters 43

Baked Apricots with Honey and Almonds 129

PERFECTLY PLANT-BASED

Lean and Green Smoothie 13

Heirloom Tomato and Cucumber Salad with Peach Dressing 25

Vegan Three-Bean Chili 54

Baked Sweet Potato Wedges with Garlic Aioli 42

RAINY-DAY COMFORT FOOD

Ham and Cheese Soup 31

Pressure Cooker Beef Stew 112

Creamy Potato Salad 37

Double Chocolate Chip Cookies 122

DELECTABLE DINNER PARTY

Spicy Avocado Dip 45

Herb-Crusted Racks of Lamb 108

Bacon-Wrapped Asparagus, Sweet Peppers, and Green Beans 36

Chocolate Mousse with Fresh Whipped Cream 120

BREAKFAST FOR DINNER

Baked Avocado Egg Boats 15

Vegetable Frittata 17

Belgian Waffles 19

Hawaiian Smoothie Bowl 12

MEASUREMENT CONVERSIONS

VOLUME EQUIVALENTS (LIQUID)

US STANDARD	US STANDARD (OUNCES)	METRIC (APPROXIMATE)
2 tablespoons	1 fl. oz.	30 mL
¼ cup	2 fl. oz.	60 mL
½ cup	4 fl. oz.	120 mL
1 cup	8 fl. oz.	240 mL
1½ cups	12 fl. oz.	355 mL
2 cups or 1 pint	16 fl. oz.	475 mL
4 cups or 1 quart	32 fl. oz.	1 L
1 gallon	128 fl. oz.	4 L

OVEN TEMPERATURES

FAHRENHEIT	CELSIUS (APPROXIMATE)
250°F	120°C
300°F	150°C
325°F	165°C
350°F	180°C
375°F	190°C
400°F	200°C
425°F	220°C
450°F	230°C

VOLUME EQUIVALENTS (DRY)

US STANDARD	METRIC (APPROXIMATE)
⅛ teaspoon	0.5 mL
¼ teaspoon	1 mL
½ teaspoon	2 mL
¾ teaspoon	4 mL
1 teaspoon	5 mL
1 tablespoon	15 mL
¼ cup	59 mL
⅓ cup	79 mL
½ cup	118 mL
⅔ cup	156 mL
¾ cup	177 mL
1 cup	235 mL
2 cups or 1 pint	475 mL
3 cups	700 mL
4 cups or 1 quart	1 L

WEIGHT EQUIVALENTS

US STANDARD	METRIC (APPROXIMATE)
½ ounce	15 g
1 ounce	30 g
2 ounces	60 g
4 ounces	115 g
8 ounces	225 g
12 ounces	340 g
16 ounces or 1 pound	455 g

RESOURCES

Beyond Celiac (beyondceliac.org): A nonprofit organization for celiac disease.

Celiac Disease Foundation (celiac.org): A nonprofit organization that raises awareness about gluten sensitivities and celiac disease.

The Gluten Free (theglutenfree.com): This is my primary gluten-free recipe blog with more than 700 delicious recipes.

Gluten Free by Jan (glutenfreebyjan.com): My gluten-free blog featuring more than 300 gluten-free recipes.

Harvard Health Publishing (health.harvard.edu): Publishes results of health testing on celiac disease, gluten sensitivity, and other related health problems.

National Celiac Association (nationalceliac.org): A nonprofit organization dedicated to educating and advocating for individuals with celiac disease and non-celiac gluten sensitivities.

INDEX

A

Allergies, 9
All-Purpose Dry Rub, 133
Almond butter
- Apple Sandwiches with Almond Butter, Chocolate Chips, and Granola, 48

Apples
- Apple Sandwiches with Almond Butter, Chocolate Chips, and Granola, 48
- Candied Apple Skewers, 126
- Lean and Green Smoothie, 13

Apricots
- Baked Apricots with Honey and Almonds, 129
- Grilled Pork Tenderloin with Fruit Salsa, 105

Asian Chicken Lettuce Wraps, 93
Asparagus
- Bacon-Wrapped Asparagus, Sweet Peppers, and Green Beans, 36

Avocados
- Baked Avocado Egg Boats, 15
- Egg Muffins, 16
- Quinoa Salad with Mango and Avocado, 27
- Spicy Avocado Dip, 45

B

Bacon
- Bacon and Cheese Frittata, 18
- Bacon-Wrapped Asparagus, Sweet Peppers, and Green Beans, 36
- Baked Avocado Egg Boats, 15
- Chicken Tender Nachos, 90
- Chicken with Garlic, Bacon, and Thyme, 84

Baked Apricots with Honey and Almonds, 129
Baked Avocado Egg Boats, 15
Baked Salmon with Lemon Butter and Pineapple Salsa, 79
Baked Salmon with Tomatoes and Olives, 81
Baked Sweet Potato Wedges with Garlic Aioli, 42
Bananas
- Hawaiian Smoothie Bowl, 12

Barbecue Meat Loaf, 114
Barbecue Sauce, 139
Basic No-Knead Pizza Crust, 140
Bean Burgers, 61
Bean curd
- Thai Stir-Fried Noodles with Roasted Peanuts, 59
- Vegetarian Casserole, 69

Bean Dip, 38
Beans
- Bean Burgers, 61
- Bean Dip, 38
- Chicken and Mango Salad in Lettuce Bowls, 26
- Easy Taco Soup, 32
- Mexican Chili Corn Pie, 56
- Minestrone Pasta Salad, 28
- Quinoa Salad with Mango and Avocado, 27
- Southern Rice and Beans, 55
- Vegan Three-Bean Chili, 54

Bean sprouts
- Thai Stir-Fried Noodles with Roasted Peanuts, 59

Beef
- Barbecue Meat Loaf, 114
- Easy Sloppy Joes, 113
- Easy Taco Soup, 32
- Grilled Loaded Flank Steaks with Corn Salsa, 109
- Grilled Steaks with Mushroom Sauce, 110–111
- Hamburger with Mushroom and Fusilli Pasta, 115
- Pressure Cooker Beef Stew, 112
- steak doneness, 111
- Szechuan Beef with Snow Peas, 117
- Teriyaki Beef with Rice Noodles, 116

Belgian Waffles, 19
Berries
- Berry-Chia Yogurt Parfait, 14
- Berry Crepes, 20
- Lemon Curd with Mixed Berries, 127
- Pistachio Cranberry Energy Bites, 44

Blackened Salmon with Tomato Salsa, 78
Braised Shrimp with Vegetables, 72
Broccoli
- Braised Shrimp with Vegetables, 72
- Ham and Cheese Soup, 31
- Soba Noodles with Mushrooms, Broccoli, and Tofu, 58
- Tofu and Mixed Vegetable Stir-Fry, 57
- Vegetarian Casserole, 69

C

Cabbage
- Confetti Tuna in Celery Sticks, 40
- Pork and Pineapple Stir-Fry, 103
- Shrimp and Snow Pea Stir-Fry with Cashews, 75

Candied Apple Skewers, 126

Carrots
- Chicken and Wild Rice Soup, 33
- Confetti Tuna in Celery Sticks, 40
- Fast Chicken Fried Rice, 96
- Orzo-Mushroom Pilaf, 68
- Pork and Pineapple Stir-Fry, 103
- Pressure Cooker Beef Stew, 112
- Shrimp and Snow Pea Stir-Fry with Cashews, 75
- Tofu and Mixed Vegetable Stir-Fry, 57
- Vegetable Fritters, 43
- Vegetarian Casserole, 69
- Veggie and Pineapple Fried Rice, 60

Cauliflower
- Margherita Pizza with Cauliflower Crust, 64

Celery
- Chicken and Wild Rice Soup, 33
- Confetti Tuna in Celery Sticks, 40
- Creamy Potato Salad, 37
- Garden Gazpacho Soup, 29
- Mexican Chili Corn Pie, 56
- Shrimp and Snow Pea Stir-Fry with Cashews, 75

Celiac disease, 2

Cheese. *See also* Cream cheese; Ricotta cheese
- Bacon and Cheese Frittata, 18
- Barbecue Meat Loaf, 114
- Bean Burgers, 61
- Bean Dip, 38
- Cheesy Chicken Wings, 86
- Chicken and Mango Salad in Lettuce Bowls, 26
- Chicken Tender Nachos, 90
- Creamy Pasta with Spinach and Pecans, 63
- Easy Sloppy Joes, 113
- Egg Muffins, 16
- Ham and Cheese Soup, 31
- Margherita Pizza with Cauliflower Crust, 64
- Mexican Chili Corn Pie, 56
- Minestrone Pasta Salad, 28
- Mushroom Stroganoff, 67
- Pepper Jack–Stuffed Chicken, 92
- Polenta with Sautéed Mushrooms, 65–66
- Roasted Corn on the Cob with Parmesan Cheese, 50
- Saucy Shrimp with Spaghetti, 73
- Skillet Veggie Lasagna, 62
- Vegetable Frittata, 17
- Vegetarian Casserole, 69
- Watermelon-Tomato Salad, 24
- Zucchini Pizza Bites, 49

Cheesy Chicken Wings, 86

Chia seeds
- Berry-Chia Yogurt Parfait, 14
- Pistachio Cranberry Energy Bites, 44

Chicken
- Asian Chicken Lettuce Wraps, 93
- Cheesy Chicken Wings, 86
- Chicken and Mango Salad in Lettuce Bowls, 26
- Chicken and Wild Rice Soup, 33
- Chicken Tender Nachos, 90
- Chicken with Garlic, Bacon, and Thyme, 84
- Fast Chicken Fried Rice, 96
- Garlicky Broiled Chicken Thighs, 85
- Grilled Chicken with Pineapple-Ginger Glaze, 94
- Pepper Jack–Stuffed Chicken, 92
- Popcorn Chicken with Mashed Potatoes and Gravy, 88–89
- Sheet-Pan Chicken Fajitas, 91
- Sweet-and-Sour Chicken Stir-Fry, 95
- Sweet-and-Spicy Barbecue Chicken, 87
- Teriyaki Chicken Burgers, 97

Chickpeas
- Minestrone Pasta Salad, 28

Chocolate, 4
- Apple Sandwiches with Almond Butter, Chocolate Chips, and Granola, 48
- Chocolate Mousse with Fresh Whipped Cream, 120
- Churros with Chocolate Dipping Sauce, 123
- Double Chocolate Chip Cookies, 122
- Gooey Turtle Bars, 121
- No-Bake Protein Energy Balls, 47
- Pistachio Cranberry Energy Bites, 44

Churros with Chocolate Dipping Sauce, 123

Coconut
- Marvelous Coconut Macaroons, 124
- No-Bake Protein Energy Balls, 47

Confetti Tuna in Celery Sticks, 40

Corn, 3
- Chicken and Mango Salad in Lettuce Bowls, 26
- Easy Taco Soup, 32
- Grilled Loaded Flank Steaks with Corn Salsa, 109
- Mexican Chili Corn Pie, 56
- Roasted Corn on the Cob with Parmesan Cheese, 50

Cornmeal
- Mexican Chili Corn Pie, 56
- Polenta with Sautéed Mushrooms, 65–66
- Quick Sausage Cornmeal Pancakes, 21

Cream cheese
- Bean Dip, 38
- Berry Crepes, 20
- Confetti Tuna in Celery Sticks, 40
- Creamy Pasta with Spinach and Pecans, 63
- Cucumber Cups with Sun-Dried Tomato and Cream Cheese, 39

Creamy Pasta with Spinach and Pecans, 63

Creamy Potato Salad, 37

Cross-contamination, 4

Cucumbers
- Chicken and Mango Salad in Lettuce Bowls, 26
- Cucumber Cups with Sun-Dried Tomato and Cream Cheese, 39
- Grilled Loaded Flank Steaks with Corn Salsa, 109
- Heirloom Tomato and Cucumber Salad with Peach Dressing, 25

D

Dairy-free
- All-Purpose Dry Rub, 133
- Apple Sandwiches with Almond Butter, Chocolate Chips, and Granola, 48
- Asian Chicken Lettuce Wraps, 93
- Bacon-Wrapped Asparagus, Sweet Peppers, and Green Beans, 36
- Baked Avocado Egg Boats, 15
- Baked Salmon with Tomatoes and Olives, 81
- Baked Sweet Potato Wedges with Garlic Aioli, 42
- Barbecue Sauce, 139
- Basic No-Knead Pizza Crust, 140
- Blackened Salmon with Tomato Salsa, 78
- Braised Shrimp with Vegetables, 72
- Chicken and Wild Rice Soup, 33
- Fresh Roasted Tomato Sauce, 136
- Garden Gazpacho Soup, 29
- Grilled Chicken with Pineapple-Ginger Glaze, 94
- Grilled Lime and Chili Pork Chops, 102
- Grilled Loaded Flank Steaks with Corn Salsa, 109
- Grilled Pork Tenderloin with Fruit Salsa, 105
- Heirloom Tomato and Cucumber Salad with Peach Dressing, 25
- Herb-Crusted Racks of Lamb, 108
- Homemade Cajun Seasoning, 134
- Italian Seasoning, 132
- Lean and Green Smoothie, 13
- Lime and Thyme Tuna Steaks, 77
- No-Bake Protein Energy Balls, 47
- Pistachio Cranberry Energy Bites, 44
- Pork and Pineapple Stir-Fry, 103
- Pressure Cooker Beef Stew, 112

Dairy-free (continued)
- Rosemary-Garlic and Citrus Marinated Grilled Lamb Chops, 107
- Shrimp and Pineapple Curry, 74
- Shrimp and Snow Pea Stir-Fry with Cashews, 75
- Soba Noodles with Mushrooms, Broccoli, and Tofu, 58
- Southern Rice and Beans, 55
- Spicy Avocado Dip, 45
- Sweet-and-Sour Chicken Stir-Fry, 95
- Sweet-and-Sour Sauce, 138
- Sweet-and-Sour Zucchini, 46
- Szechuan Beef with Snow Peas, 117
- Tapioca Pudding, 125
- Teriyaki Beef with Rice Noodles, 116
- Teriyaki Chicken Burgers, 97
- Thai Stir-Fried Noodles with Roasted Peanuts, 59
- Thick Teriyaki Sauce, 135
- Tofu and Mixed Vegetable Stir-Fry, 57
- Turkey Cutlets with Pepper and Tomato Ragout, 98
- Vegan Three-Bean Chili, 54
- Vegetable Fritters, 43
- Veggie and Pineapple Fried Rice, 60

Dairy products, 9

Dates
- Pistachio Cranberry Energy Bites, 44

Desserts
- Baked Apricots with Honey and Almonds, 129
- Candied Apple Skewers, 126
- Chocolate Mousse with Fresh Whipped Cream, 120
- Churros with Chocolate Dipping Sauce, 123
- Double Chocolate Chip Cookies, 122
- Fresh Peach Cobbler, 128
- Gooey Turtle Bars, 121
- Lemon Curd with Mixed Berries, 127
- Marvelous Coconut Macaroons, 124
- Tapioca Pudding, 125

Dips and spreads
- Bean Dip, 38
- Spicy Avocado Dip, 45
- Vegetable Dip, 41

Double Chocolate Chip Cookies, 122

E

Easy Sloppy Joes, 113

Easy Taco Soup, 32

Eggs, 9
- Bacon and Cheese Frittata, 18
- Baked Avocado Egg Boats, 15
- Chocolate Mousse with Fresh Whipped Cream, 120
- Creamy Potato Salad, 37
- Egg Muffins, 16
- Fast Chicken Fried Rice, 96
- Lemon Curd with Mixed Berries, 127
- Marvelous Coconut Macaroons, 124
- Vegetable Frittata, 17

Equipment, 7

F

Fast Chicken Fried Rice, 96

Fish, 9
- Baked Salmon with Lemon Butter and Pineapple Salsa, 79
- Baked Salmon with Tomatoes and Olives, 81
- Blackened Salmon with Tomato Salsa, 78
- Confetti Tuna in Celery Sticks, 40
- Lime and Thyme Tuna Steaks, 77
- Pan-Fried Tilapia with Balsamic Cherry Tomatoes, 76
- Pecan-Crusted Salmon, 80

Food allergies, 9

Fresh Peach Cobbler, 128

Fresh Roasted Tomato Sauce, 136

G

Garden Gazpacho Soup, 29

Garlicky Broiled Chicken Thighs, 85

Gluten, 2
- -free grains, 3
- sources of, 4
- swaps, 5

Gluten-Free Baking Mix, 141
Gluten sensitivities, 2
Gooey Turtle Bars, 121
Granola
Apple Sandwiches with Almond Butter, Chocolate Chips, and Granola, 48
Berry-Chia Yogurt Parfait, 14
Grapes
Lean and Green Smoothie, 13
Green beans
Bacon-Wrapped Asparagus, Sweet Peppers, and Green Beans, 36
Pressure Cooker Beef Stew, 112
Grilled Chicken with Pineapple-Ginger Glaze, 94
Grilled Lime and Chili Pork Chops, 102
Grilled Loaded Flank Steaks with Corn Salsa, 109
Grilled Pork Tenderloin with Fruit Salsa, 105
Grilled Steaks with Mushroom Sauce, 110–111

H

Ham and Cheese Soup, 31
Hamburger with Mushroom and Fusilli Pasta, 115
Hawaiian Smoothie Bowl, 12
Heirloom Tomato and Cucumber Salad with Peach Dressing, 25
Herb-Crusted Racks of Lamb, 108
Homemade Cajun Seasoning, 134

I

Italian Seasoning, 132

K

Kale
Lean and Green Smoothie, 13
Kielbasa, Potato, and Pepper Supper, 106

L

Labels, 3
Lamb
Herb-Crusted Racks of Lamb, 108
Rosemary-Garlic and Citrus Marinated Grilled Lamb Chops, 107
Lean and Green Smoothie, 13
Lemon Curd with Mixed Berries, 127
Lettuce
Asian Chicken Lettuce Wraps, 93
Chicken and Mango Salad in Lettuce Bowls, 26
Lime and Thyme Tuna Steaks, 77

M

Mangos
Chicken and Mango Salad in Lettuce Bowls, 26
Hawaiian Smoothie Bowl, 12
Quinoa Salad with Mango and Avocado, 27
Margherita Pizza with Cauliflower Crust, 64
Marvelous Coconut Macaroons, 124
Menus, 142–143
Mexican Chili Corn Pie, 56
Milk, 9
Millet, 3
Minestrone Pasta Salad, 28
Mushrooms
Braised Shrimp with Vegetables, 72
Grilled Steaks with Mushroom Sauce, 110–111
Hamburger with Mushroom and Fusilli Pasta, 115
Mushroom Stroganoff, 67
Orzo-Mushroom Pilaf, 68
Polenta with Sautéed Mushrooms, 65–66
Pressure Cooker Beef Stew, 112
Shrimp and Snow Pea Stir-Fry with Cashews, 75
Soba Noodles with Mushrooms, Broccoli, and Tofu, 58
Turkey Meat Loaf, 99

N

No-Bake Protein Energy Balls, 47
Noodles. *See also* Pasta
Soba Noodles with Mushrooms, Broccoli, and Tofu, 58
Teriyaki Beef with Rice Noodles, 116
Thai Stir-Fried Noodles with Roasted Peanuts, 59
Nut-free
All-Purpose Dry Rub, 133
Asian Chicken Lettuce Wraps, 93
Bacon and Cheese Frittata, 18

Nut-free (*continued*)
Bacon-Wrapped Asparagus, Sweet Peppers, and Green Beans, 36
Baked Avocado Egg Boats, 15
Baked Salmon with Lemon Butter and Pineapple Salsa, 79
Baked Salmon with Tomatoes and Olives, 81
Barbecue Meat Loaf, 114
Basic No-Knead Pizza Crust, 140
Bean Dip, 38
Blackened Salmon with Tomato Salsa, 78
Braised Shrimp with Vegetables, 72
Cheesy Chicken Wings, 86
Chicken and Mango Salad in Lettuce Bowls, 26
Chicken and Wild Rice Soup, 33
Chicken Tender Nachos, 90
Chocolate Mousse with Fresh Whipped Cream, 120
Confetti Tuna in Celery Sticks, 40
Creamy Potato Salad, 37
Cucumber Cups with Sun-Dried Tomato and Cream Cheese, 39
Easy Taco Soup, 32
Egg Muffins, 16
Fast Chicken Fried Rice, 96
Fresh Roasted Tomato Sauce, 136
Garlicky Broiled Chicken Thighs, 85
Grilled Chicken with Pineapple-Ginger Glaze, 94
Grilled Lime and Chili Pork Chops, 102
Grilled Loaded Flank Steaks with Corn Salsa, 109
Grilled Pork Tenderloin with Fruit Salsa, 105
Hamburger with Mushroom and Fusilli Pasta, 115
Heirloom Tomato and Cucumber Salad with Peach Dressing, 25
Herb-Crusted Racks of Lamb, 108
Homemade Cajun Seasoning, 134
Italian Seasoning, 132
Kielbasa, Potato, and Pepper Supper, 106
Lean and Green Smoothie, 13
Lime and Thyme Tuna Steaks, 77
Margherita Pizza with Cauliflower Crust, 64
Minestrone Pasta Salad, 28
Mushroom Stroganoff, 67
Old-Fashioned Potato Soup, 30
Orzo-Mushroom Pilaf, 68
Pepper Jack–Stuffed Chicken, 92
Polenta with Sautéed Mushrooms, 65–66
Popcorn Chicken with Mashed Potatoes and Gravy, 88–89
Pork and Pineapple Stir-Fry, 103
Pressure Cooker Beef Stew, 112
Quinoa Salad with Mango and Avocado, 27
Roasted Corn on the Cob with Parmesan Cheese, 50
Rosemary-Garlic and Citrus Marinated Grilled Lamb Chops, 107
Saucy Shrimp with Spaghetti, 73
Sheet-Pan Chicken Fajitas, 91
Shrimp and Pineapple Curry, 74
Skillet Pork Chops with Smashed Potatoes, 104
Skillet Veggie Lasagna, 62
Soba Noodles with Mushrooms, Broccoli, and Tofu, 58
Southern Rice and Beans, 55
Spicy Avocado Dip, 45
Sweet-and-Sour Chicken Stir-Fry, 95
Sweet-and-Sour Sauce, 138
Sweet-and-Spicy Barbecue Chicken, 87
Szechuan Beef with Snow Peas, 117
Tapioca Pudding, 125
Tartar Sauce, 137
Teriyaki Beef with Rice Noodles, 116
Teriyaki Chicken Burgers, 97

Thick Teriyaki Sauce, 135
Tofu and Mixed Vegetable Stir-Fry, 57
Turkey Cutlets with Pepper and Tomato Ragout, 98
Vegan Three-Bean Chili, 54
Vegetable Dip, 41
Vegetable Frittata, 17
Vegetable Fritters, 43
Vegetarian Casserole, 69
Veggie and Pineapple Fried Rice, 60
Watermelon-Tomato Salad, 24
Zucchini Pizza Bites, 49

Nuts
Baked Apricots with Honey and Almonds, 129
Baked Sweet Potato Wedges with Garlic Aioli, 42
Candied Apple Skewers, 126
Creamy Pasta with Spinach and Pecans, 63
Gooey Turtle Bars, 121
No-Bake Protein Energy Balls, 47
peanuts, 9
Pecan-Crusted Salmon, 80
Pistachio Cranberry Energy Bites, 44
Quick Sausage Cornmeal Pancakes, 21
Shrimp and Snow Pea Stir-Fry with Cashews, 75
Thai Stir-Fried Noodles with Roasted Peanuts, 59
tree, 9

O

Oats
No-Bake Protein Energy Balls, 47
Pistachio Cranberry Energy Bites, 44
Old-Fashioned Potato Soup, 30
Olives
Baked Salmon with Tomatoes and Olives, 81
Cucumber Cups with Sun-Dried Tomato and Cream Cheese, 39
Minestrone Pasta Salad, 28
Orzo-Mushroom Pilaf, 68

P

Pan-Fried Tilapia with Balsamic Cherry Tomatoes, 76
Pantry staples, 8
Pasta
Creamy Pasta with Spinach and Pecans, 63
Hamburger with Mushroom and Fusilli Pasta, 115
Minestrone Pasta Salad, 28
Mushroom Stroganoff, 67
Orzo-Mushroom Pilaf, 68
Saucy Shrimp with Spaghetti, 73
Skillet Veggie Lasagna, 62
Peaches
Fresh Peach Cobbler, 128
Grilled Pork Tenderloin with Fruit Salsa, 105
Heirloom Tomato and Cucumber Salad with Peach Dressing, 25
Peanut butter
No-Bake Protein Energy Balls, 47
Peas
Braised Shrimp with Vegetables, 72
Creamy Pasta with Spinach and Pecans, 63
Shrimp and Snow Pea Stir-Fry with Cashews, 75
Szechuan Beef with Snow Peas, 117
Tofu and Mixed Vegetable Stir-Fry, 57
Pecan-Crusted Salmon, 80
Pepper Jack–Stuffed Chicken, 92
Pepperoni
Zucchini Pizza Bites, 49
Peppers
Bacon-Wrapped Asparagus, Sweet Peppers, and Green Beans, 36
Bean Dip, 38
Blackened Salmon with Tomato Salsa, 78
Chicken and Mango Salad in Lettuce Bowls, 26
Chicken Tender Nachos, 90
Easy Sloppy Joes, 113
Easy Taco Soup, 32
Garden Gazpacho Soup, 29
Grilled Loaded Flank Steaks with Corn Salsa, 109
Kielbasa, Potato, and Pepper Supper, 106
Mexican Chili Corn Pie, 56
Quinoa Salad with Mango and Avocado, 27
Sheet-Pan Chicken Fajitas, 91
Skillet Veggie Lasagna, 62
Southern Rice and Beans, 55

Peppers (*continued*)
Sweet-and-Sour Zucchini, 46
Thai Stir-Fried Noodles with Roasted Peanuts, 59
Tofu and Mixed Vegetable Stir-Fry, 57
Turkey Cutlets with Pepper and Tomato Ragout, 98
Vegan Three-Bean Chili, 54
Vegetable Dip, 41
Vegetable Frittata, 17
Pineapple
Baked Salmon with Lemon Butter and Pineapple Salsa, 79
Grilled Chicken with Pineapple-Ginger Glaze, 94
Hawaiian Smoothie Bowl, 12
Lean and Green Smoothie, 13
Pork and Pineapple Stir-Fry, 103
Shrimp and Pineapple Curry, 74
Veggie and Pineapple Fried Rice, 60
Pistachio Cranberry Energy Bites, 44
Pizzas
Basic No-Knead Pizza Crust, 140
Margherita Pizza with Cauliflower Crust, 64
Zucchini Pizza Bites, 49
Plums
Grilled Pork Tenderloin with Fruit Salsa, 105
Polenta with Sautéed Mushrooms, 65–66
Popcorn Chicken with Mashed Potatoes and Gravy, 88–89
Pork. *See also* Bacon; Ham; Sausage
Grilled Lime and Chili Pork Chops, 102
Grilled Pork Tenderloin with Fruit Salsa, 105
Pork and Pineapple Stir-Fry, 103
Skillet Pork Chops with Smashed Potatoes, 104
Potatoes. *See also* Sweet potatoes
Creamy Potato Salad, 37
Ham and Cheese Soup, 31
Kielbasa, Potato, and Pepper Supper, 106
Old-Fashioned Potato Soup, 30
Popcorn Chicken with Mashed Potatoes and Gravy, 88–89
Pressure Cooker Beef Stew, 112
Skillet Pork Chops with Smashed Potatoes, 104
Vegetable Fritters, 43
Vegetarian Casserole, 69
Pressure Cooker Beef Stew, 112

Q

Quick Sausage Cornmeal Pancakes, 21
Quinoa, 3
Quinoa Salad with Mango and Avocado, 27

R

Rice, 3
Chicken and Wild Rice Soup, 33
Fast Chicken Fried Rice, 96
Shrimp and Pineapple Curry, 74
Southern Rice and Beans, 55
Veggie and Pineapple Fried Rice, 60
Ricotta cheese
Skillet Veggie Lasagna, 62
Roasted Corn on the Cob with Parmesan Cheese, 50
Rosemary-Garlic and Citrus Marinated Grilled Lamb Chops, 107

S

Salads
Chicken and Mango Salad in Lettuce Bowls, 26
Creamy Potato Salad, 37
Heirloom Tomato and Cucumber Salad with Peach Dressing, 25
Minestrone Pasta Salad, 28
Quinoa Salad with Mango and Avocado, 27
Watermelon-Tomato Salad, 24
Salmon
Baked Salmon with Lemon Butter and Pineapple Salsa, 79
Baked Salmon with Tomatoes and Olives, 81

Blackened Salmon with Tomato Salsa, 78
Pecan-Crusted Salmon, 80
Sauces
Barbecue Sauce, 139
Fresh Roasted Tomato Sauce, 136
Sweet-and-Sour Sauce, 138
Tartar Sauce, 137
Thick Teriyaki Sauce, 135
Saucy Shrimp with Spaghetti, 73
Sausage
Kielbasa, Potato, and Pepper Supper, 106
Quick Sausage Cornmeal Pancakes, 21
Seasonings
All-Purpose Dry Rub, 133
Homemade Cajun Seasoning, 134
Italian Seasoning, 132
Sheet-Pan Chicken Fajitas, 91
Shellfish, 9
Shrimp
Braised Shrimp with Vegetables, 72
Saucy Shrimp with Spaghetti, 73
Shrimp and Pineapple Curry, 74
Shrimp and Snow Pea Stir-Fry with Cashews, 75
Skillet Pork Chops with Smashed Potatoes, 104
Skillet Veggie Lasagna, 62
Smoothies
Hawaiian Smoothie Bowl, 12
Lean and Green Smoothie, 13
Soba Noodles with Mushrooms, Broccoli, and Tofu, 58
Sorghum, 3
Soups
Chicken and Wild Rice Soup, 33
Easy Taco Soup, 32
Garden Gazpacho Soup, 29
Ham and Cheese Soup, 31
Old-Fashioned Potato Soup, 30
Pressure Cooker Beef Stew, 112
Vegan Three-Bean Chili, 54
Southern Rice and Beans, 55
Soy, 9
Soy-free
All-Purpose Dry Rub, 133
Apple Sandwiches with Almond Butter, Chocolate Chips, and Granola, 48
Bacon and Cheese Frittata, 18
Baked Apricots with Honey and Almonds, 129
Baked Avocado Egg Boats, 15
Baked Sweet Potato Wedges with Garlic Aioli, 42
Bean Dip, 38
Berry-Chia Yogurt Parfait, 14
Blackened Salmon with Tomato Salsa, 78
Cheesy Chicken Wings, 86
Chicken Tender Nachos, 90
Confetti Tuna in Celery Sticks, 40
Creamy Pasta with Spinach and Pecans, 63
Cucumber Cups with Sun-Dried Tomato and Cream Cheese, 39
Egg Muffins, 16
Fresh Roasted Tomato Sauce, 136
Grilled Pork Tenderloin with Fruit Salsa, 105
Hawaiian Smoothie Bowl, 12
Heirloom Tomato and Cucumber Salad with Peach Dressing, 25
Herb-Crusted Racks of Lamb, 108
Homemade Cajun Seasoning, 134
Italian Seasoning, 132
Kielbasa, Potato, and Pepper Supper, 106
Lean and Green Smoothie, 13
Lemon Curd with Mixed Berries, 127
Lime and Thyme Tuna Steaks, 77
Margherita Pizza with Cauliflower Crust, 64
Marvelous Coconut Macaroons, 124
No-Bake Protein Energy Balls, 47
Old-Fashioned Potato Soup, 30
Pecan-Crusted Salmon, 80
Pistachio Cranberry Energy Bites, 44
Pressure Cooker Beef Stew, 112
Quinoa Salad with Mango and Avocado, 27
Roasted Corn on the Cob with Parmesan Cheese, 50

Soy-free (*continued*)
Rosemary-Garlic and Citrus Marinated Grilled Lamb Chops, 107
Saucy Shrimp with Spaghetti, 73
Sheet-Pan Chicken Fajitas, 91
Skillet Veggie Lasagna, 62
Southern Rice and Beans, 55
Spicy Avocado Dip, 45
Tapioca Pudding, 125
Turkey Cutlets with Pepper and Tomato Ragout, 98
Vegetable Frittata, 17
Vegetable Fritters, 43
Watermelon-Tomato Salad, 24
Spicy Avocado Dip, 45
Spinach
Creamy Pasta with Spinach and Pecans, 63
Egg Muffins, 16
Skillet Veggie Lasagna, 62
Substitutions and swaps, 5, 9
Sweet-and-Sour Chicken Stir-Fry, 95
Sweet-and-Sour Sauce, 138
Sweet-and-Sour Zucchini, 46
Sweet-and-Spicy Barbecue Chicken, 87
Sweet Potato Wedges, Baked, with Garlic Aioli, 42
Szechuan Beef with Snow Peas, 117

T

Tapioca Pudding, 125
Tartar Sauce, 137
Teff, 3
Teriyaki Beef with Rice Noodles, 116
Teriyaki Chicken Burgers, 97
Thai Stir-Fried Noodles with Roasted Peanuts, 59
Thick Teriyaki Sauce, 135
Tilapia, Pan-Fried, with Balsamic Cherry Tomatoes, 76
Tofu
Soba Noodles with Mushrooms, Broccoli, and Tofu, 58
Tofu and Mixed Vegetable Stir-Fry, 57
Tomatoes
Baked Salmon with Tomatoes and Olives, 81
Bean Dip, 38
Blackened Salmon with Tomato Salsa, 78
Cucumber Cups with Sun-Dried Tomato and Cream Cheese, 39
Easy Taco Soup, 32
Egg Muffins, 16
Fresh Roasted Tomato Sauce, 136
Garden Gazpacho Soup, 29
Grilled Loaded Flank Steaks with Corn Salsa, 109
Heirloom Tomato and Cucumber Salad with Peach Dressing, 25
Margherita Pizza with Cauliflower Crust, 64
Mexican Chili Corn Pie, 56
Minestrone Pasta Salad, 28
Pan-Fried Tilapia with Balsamic Cherry Tomatoes, 76
Saucy Shrimp with Spaghetti, 73
Skillet Veggie Lasagna, 62
Southern Rice and Beans, 55
Szechuan Beef with Snow Peas, 117
Turkey Cutlets with Pepper and Tomato Ragout, 98
Vegan Three-Bean Chili, 54
Watermelon-Tomato Salad, 24
Tuna
Confetti Tuna in Celery Sticks, 40
Lime and Thyme Tuna Steaks, 77
Turkey Cutlets with Pepper and Tomato Ragout, 98
Turkey Meat Loaf, 99

V

Vegan
All-Purpose Dry Rub, 133
Apple Sandwiches with Almond Butter, Chocolate Chips, and Granola, 48
Baked Sweet Potato Wedges with Garlic Aioli, 42
Gluten-Free Baking Mix, 141
Heirloom Tomato and Cucumber Salad with Peach Dressing, 25

Homemade Cajun Seasoning, 134
Italian Seasoning, 132
Lean and Green Smoothie, 13
Soba Noodles with Mushrooms, Broccoli, and Tofu, 58
Southern Rice and Beans, 55
Spicy Avocado Dip, 45
Sweet-and-Sour Sauce, 138
Sweet-and-Sour Zucchini, 46
Tapioca Pudding, 125
Thai Stir-Fried Noodles with Roasted Peanuts, 59
Thick Teriyaki Sauce, 135
Tofu and Mixed Vegetable Stir-Fry, 57
Vegan Three-Bean Chili, 54
Vegetable Dip, 41
Vegetable Frittata, 17
Vegetable Fritters, 43
Vegetables. *See also specific*
Sweet-and-Sour Chicken Stir-Fry, 95
Vegetarian. *See also* Vegan
Baked Apricots with Honey and Almonds, 129
Basic No-Knead Pizza Crust, 140
Bean Burgers, 61
Bean Dip, 38
Belgian Waffles, 19
Berry-Chia Yogurt Parfait, 14
Berry Crepes, 20
Candied Apple Skewers, 126
Chocolate Mousse with Fresh Whipped Cream, 120
Churros with Chocolate Dipping Sauce, 123
Creamy Pasta with Spinach and Pecans, 63
Creamy Potato Salad, 37
Cucumber Cups with Sun-Dried Tomato and Cream Cheese, 39
Double Chocolate Chip Cookies, 122
Egg Muffins, 16
Fresh Peach Cobbler, 128
Gooey Turtle Bars, 121
Hawaiian Smoothie Bowl, 12
Lemon Curd with Mixed Berries, 127
Margherita Pizza with Cauliflower Crust, 64
Marvelous Coconut Macaroons, 124
Mexican Chili Corn Pie, 56
Minestrone Pasta Salad, 28
Mushroom Stroganoff, 67
No-Bake Protein Energy Balls, 47
Old-Fashioned Potato Soup, 30
Orzo-Mushroom Pilaf, 68
Pistachio Cranberry Energy Bites, 44
Polenta with Sautéed Mushrooms, 65–66
Roasted Corn on the Cob with Parmesan Cheese, 50
Skillet Veggie Lasagna, 62
Tartar Sauce, 137
Vegetable Dip, 41
Vegetable Frittata, 17
Vegetable Fritters, 43
Vegetarian Casserole, 69
Veggie and Pineapple Fried Rice, 60
Watermelon-Tomato Salad, 24
Vegetarian Casserole, 69
Veggie and Pineapple Fried Rice, 60

W

Watercress
Watermelon-Tomato Salad, 24
Watermelon-Tomato Salad, 24

Y

Yogurt
Berry-Chia Yogurt Parfait, 14
Confetti Tuna in Celery Sticks, 40
Hawaiian Smoothie Bowl, 12
Quick Sausage Cornmeal Pancakes, 21

Z

Zucchini
Confetti Tuna in Celery Sticks, 40
Creamy Potato Salad, 37
Fast Chicken Fried Rice, 96
Kielbasa, Potato, and Pepper Supper, 106
Skillet Veggie Lasagna, 62
Sweet-and-Sour Zucchini, 46
Tofu and Mixed Vegetable Stir-Fry, 57
Vegan Three-Bean Chili, 54
Vegetable Frittata, 17
Vegetable Fritters, 43
Veggie and Pineapple Fried Rice, 60
Zucchini Pizza Bites, 49

ACKNOWLEDGMENTS

Many thanks go out to my friends and family who encouraged and inspired me, especially my dear husband, Bill, who sometimes pushes me to do things I want to accomplish but am afraid to try; my two sons, Brandon and Jacob, who sampled my cooking; and my very close friend Vikki Mata, who has always supported me.

To my extended family in New York, my sister, Jovy, who shared some ideas, and my in-laws Mr. and Mrs. Frederic Withington, who also tasted and sampled my cooking.

To the amazing editors and the whole crew at Callisto Media, I am ever grateful! This book would not ever have happened without you. Thank you!

ABOUT THE AUTHOR

Jan Withington is the creator of TheGlutenFree.com and GlutenFreeByJan.com. She is a former grade-school teacher in the Philippines and a licensed substitute teacher in Oregon. After experiencing a mysterious burning pain in her side for years, she was eventually diagnosed with gluten intolerance and food allergies. She has spent years experimenting with and developing gluten-free recipes that she and her whole family loves. She and her husband live in Portland, Oregon.

CPSIA information can be obtained
at www.ICGtesting.com
Printed in the USA
JSHW032234040121
10700JS00004B/181

9 781646 118250